The Abortion Issue

ISSUES
(formerly Issues for the Nineties)

Volume 34

Editor

Craig Donnellan

Independence
Educational Publishers
Cambridge

First published by Independence
PO Box 295
Cambridge CB1 3XP
England

British Library Cataloguing in Publication Data
The Abortion Issue – (Issues Series)
I. Donnellan, Craig II. Series
363.4'6

ISBN 1 86168 143 7

Printed in Great Britain
The Burlington Press
Cambridge

Typeset by
Claire Boyd

Cover
The illustration on the front cover is by Pumpkin House.

CONTENTS

Chapter One: An Overview

Chapter Two: The Right to Choose?

Introduction

The Abortion Issue is the thirty-fourth volume in the **Issues** series. The aim of this series is to offer up-to-date information about important issues in our world.

The Abortion Issue looks at the arguments for and against abortion.

The information comes from a wide variety of sources and includes:
Government reports and statistics
Newspaper reports and features
Magazine articles and surveys
Literature from lobby groups
and charitable organisations.

It is hoped that, as you read about the many aspects of the issues explored in this book, you will critically evaluate the information presented. It is important that you decide whether you are being presented with facts or opinions. Does the writer give a biased or an unbiased report? If an opinion is being expressed, do you agree with the writer?

The Abortion Issue offers a useful starting-point for those who need convenient access to information about the many issues involved. However, it is only a starting-point. At the back of the book is a list of organisations which you may want to contact for further information.

*****

Abortion facts

Information from Marie Stopes International

Abortion is allowed for these reasons

- Risk to life of woman
- To prevent grave permanent injury to physical or mental health of woman
- Risk of injury to physical or mental health of pregnant woman (up to 24 weeks)
- Risk of injury to the physical or mental health of existing children (up to 24 weeks)
- Substantial risk of child being born seriously handicapped

When do most abortions take place?

Abortion was legalised in 1967 in the UK and is allowed up to 24 weeks, but could happen later in rare cases, such as to save the woman's life.

In 1998, 89% of abortions were carried out before the 12th week of pregnancy.

How many?

177,332 abortions were carried out in England & Wales in 1998. 9,800 of those women came from overseas, or from elsewhere in the British Isles, such as the Irish Republic, or Northern Ireland, where abortion is illegal.

Who has an abortion?

Women of all ages, religions and cultures have abortions. Some have no children, others already have families. Most were using family planning but maybe had an accident with their contraceptive method or didn't use it properly.

Women have abortions for all sorts of reasons.

These include:

- having financial problems
- being single and lacking support
- being homeless
- having a family already
- not wanting children at all
- being pregnant as a result of incest or rape
- having relationship problems
- having a pregnancy which will result in a seriously handicapped baby.

How is abortion done?

Most abortions (those up to 12 weeks) are carried out by removing the contents of the uterus by gentle suction. This can be done under local or general anaesthetic and takes about 10 minutes. Later abortions involve gently opening the neck of the uterus (cervix) and removing the contents with an instrument.

Women who are less than nine weeks pregnant can choose the abortion pill (RU486). This causes them to have a miscarriage, but can take about six hours.

What does it cost?

In the UK, about half of all abortions are carried out on the National Health Service (NHS), which involves no cost. But a lot of women cannot get an NHS abortion because their health authority does not provide them, or because the waiting lists are too long. They may come to a charity such as Marie Stopes, where an abortion costs £335 upwards, depending on how many weeks pregnant the woman is.

Who approves an abortion?

A woman has to see two doctors to get permission, to check she understands her decision and is eligible. She does not have to see her own GP if she doesn't want him or her to know. She does not have to tell anyone except the clinic staff. If you are under 16 you should have the permission of a parent or guardian, but if this is not possible, a doctor can sometimes take responsibility.

• The above is information from Marie Stopes International. See page 41 for address details.

Answering young people's questions on abortion

Information from Brook Advisory Centres

What is an abortion?

The word abortion means ending pregnancy so that it does not result in the birth of a child. A miscarriage (or spontaneous abortion) happens naturally. An induced abortion is caused deliberately.

What is a legal abortion?

An abortion is legal if two doctors agree that it is necessary for one or more of the following reasons:

a) If the pregnancy is less than 24 weeks – if having the baby would harm the woman's mental or physical health more than having the abortion (the effect another baby would have on the health of any children she has already may be considered).

b) At any time in pregnancy – if the abortion is necessary to save the woman's life or to prevent serious permanent harm to hep mental or physical health; if there is a high risk that the baby would be seriously handicapped.

Who can have an abortion?

Any woman or girl, married or single, can have an abortion if the reason is one of those outlined in the law and two doctors sign the form.

When can a woman have an abortion?

A pregnancy test should be done as soon as a woman has missed a period and this will confirm whether she is pregnant or not. An abortion can be carried out as soon as a woman knows she is pregnant and she is sure she does not want the pregnancy to continue. Very early abortions can therefore take place soon after the woman has missed her first period.

In practice, although it is possible to get an abortion on the NHS after 12 weeks, it is very difficult and it is very rare for a doctor to perform an abortion if the pregnancy is 22 weeks or more (counting from the first day of the woman's last period). An ultrasound scan is used so that a doctor can find out the exact age of the foetus.

Where are abortions carried out and who does them?

Abortions must be carried out by a qualified doctor in an NHS hospital or in a clinic or nursing home that has been approved for abortions by the Department of Health.

Can a doctor refuse to do an abortion?

The law says that no doctor or nurse need help with an abortion if she or he has a moral objection to abortion.

Doctors who have strong personal feelings that abortion is wrong should explain this to their patient as soon as they discover that this is what she is considering. Arrangements should then be made at once for the woman to see another doctor who is willing to give advice about abortion. This may be another family doctor or a doctor who works in a local clinic.

Is it easy for a woman to get an abortion?

This will depend on her reasons for wanting an abortion, how far her pregnancy has gone, where she lives and, sometimes, whether she can afford to pay.

Abortion up to about 12 weeks of pregnancy is a relatively simple operation. After this it becomes more complicated and may be riskier to the woman, so doctors may be less willing to carry out an abortion. If a woman lives in an area where it is not easy to get an NHS abortion, it may be easier for her to pay the fees herself at a private clinic.

Where can a woman get help?

The Department of Health recommends that any pregnant woman who is not sure what to do for the best should be offered the chance to discuss the alternatives that may be available to her and help her make her own decision about what to do. This sort of help may be available through family doctors, hospitals, family planning clinics, Brook Advisory Centres or other agencies that provide pregnancy advice.

What are the choices?

A woman could decide to have the baby. She could ask for the baby to be adopted. Or she could bring up the baby with the help of the father of the child, with help from her family or on her own. If she decides to continue with the pregnancy, it is important that she sees a doctor and attends for antenatal care regularly from the start of the pregnancy, for the sake of her own health and that of the child.

If she decides she wants an abortion, she can go to her own doctor or another family doctor of her choice. She may prefer to go directly to a family planning clinic or Brook Advisory Centre or another agency set up to provide pregnancy advice. The doctor she sees will examine her to confirm she is pregnant and will discuss the effect having a baby would have on her life. If the doctor agrees that her reasons for needing an abortion are within the law, he or she will sign the certificate and send her to another doctor for a second opinion.

This may be a doctor at an NHS hospital, or at a clinic or nursing home outside the NHS. In some parts of the country, the NHS has arranged with non-NHS services, such as British Pregnancy Advisory Service or Marie Stopes Centres, to provide abortions free of charge.

How much does it cost?

The NHS provides a free service but in most areas this does not cover all women having abortions. However, she will frequently have to wait between two and four weeks and this free service is not often available beyond 12 weeks of pregnancy.

Some women choose to use a clinic run by an abortion charity or a private clinic to avoid having to wait. Fees vary from about £300 for an abortion up to 14 weeks of pregnancy, to about £500.

Is it confidential?

Anything a woman says to her doctor is treated as confidential, even if she is under 16. This means they will not tell anyone else what has been discussed. Staff working with doctors at a clinic or advice centre also keep everything confidential.

Many women find it helpful to talk about a problem pregnancy with someone they know and trust. This may be the father of the baby, a family member or close friend. In this case the woman would need to ask them to respect her confidence and not talk to anyone else about it.

Does a girl under 16 need her parents' consent for an abortion?

If a girl under 16 can show she understands what is involved she may give her own consent. The doctor will encourage the girl to involve her parents because she will need support and someone she can confide in at this time.

In practice, some doctors are not prepared to do an abortion for a girl under 16 without the consent of her parents. There may be exceptional circumstances when the girl is not prepared to tell a parent. The doctor will then have to decide whether the girl is mature enough to understand what she is doing and that it is in her best interest to have an abortion without her parent's consent. If the doctor does not think the girl has enough understanding, he or she will need the parent or guardian's consent.

Anyone of 16 or over has the right to consent to her own medical treatment including abortion.

Does the woman's own doctor have to give consent?

This is not necessary, nor does her own doctor have to be told. However, she will be advised to tell her own doctor in case his or her help is needed later. If a woman goes to a hospital or clinic as a day-care patient then a doctor in the area where she spends the night (which might be her own doctor) should be told in case she needs emergency treatment during the night.

Does the father of the child have to give consent?

According to the law, his consent is not needed. However, in most cases a woman would want to discuss the pregnancy with the man who made her pregnant.

How are abortions carried out?

1. Early abortions

If an abortion is carried out in the first nine weeks of pregnancy (counting from the first day of the last period) a woman can be given an abortion pill (mifepristone) and a drug called prostaglandin. This is called a medical abortion because it does not involve surgery. After taking the mifepristone pill she would have to return to the hospital or clinic 36 to 48 hours later to have a tablet of prostaglandin placed in her vagina. These two drugs will end most early pregnancies within the following four hours. It feels like having a heavy and rather painful period.

Most abortions before 13 weeks of pregnancy are by vacuum aspiration (the suction method). For this method the woman has either a general or a local anaesthetic. The abortion is performed through the vagina and there is no wound and no stitches. The narrow passage from the vagina through the cervix (the entrance to the uterus that is at the inner end of the vagina) is slowly stretched until it is wide enough to allow a suction tube, 8 to 12mm wide, to be passed into the inside of the uterus. It then takes only a minute to remove the pregnancy by suction. Healthy women take only an hour or so to recover and most go home the same day.

2. Later abortions

The usual method of abortion after 13 weeks is to give the woman a drug called prostaglandin in a tablet placed in the vagina. This makes the uterus contract and these contractions slowly stretch the cervix open and expel the pregnancy into the vagina. The labour that results lasts several hours. Sometimes mifepristone is also given up to two days before the prostaglandin, to shorten the time in labour and reduce the amount of prostaglandin needed. Women are given pain relief but do not need a general anaesthetic. They are looked after by an experienced and sympathetic nurse and are usually given a single room.

Some later abortions are done by dilatation and evacuation. A general anaesthetic is used and, working through the vagina, the cervix is dilated (stretched open) until an instrument can be passed into the uterus to remove the contents of the uterus in fragments. This takes 10 to 20 minutes. It is usual to spend at least one night in the hospital or nursing home.

Why do some people disagree with abortion?

People who disagree with abortion usually do so because of views they hold, such as:

- the belief that abortion, however early, involves taking a life because a new human being exists from the moment of conception;
- the feeling that the availability of abortion implies a lowered respect for human life;
- the worry that if a woman has an abortion it may make it harder for her to conceive and have a

normal pregnancy when she wants one;
- the worry that having an abortion might have a bad effect on a woman's mental health in the future;
- the fear that if abortion is available people will become lazy about using efficient contraception (birth control);
- the concern that abortion reduces the number of babies available for adoption by childless couples.

Why do others agree with abortion?

People who agree that abortion should be available hold views such as:

- the belief that a new person does not exist until the foetus is born or would survive if it was born prematurely;
- the conviction that a woman should be allowed to choose whether or not she continues with her pregnancy, particularly since early abortion involves less risk to her physical and mental health than the later stages of pregnancy and childbirth;
- the concern that every child should be wanted by his/her parents;
- the feeling that a woman should not be asked to continue with her pregnancy only to give the baby away to another couple;
- the belief that in some cases the health and wellbeing of the woman and her family may be placed at risk if she is forced to continue with the pregnancy;
- the need for abortion to be available for special cases such as pregnancy due to rape, or incest; or a pregnancy in a very young girl or a much older woman when there is more risk involved.

What does a woman have to do after an abortion?

She will be given an appointment to see a doctor about one to six weeks after the abortion to make sure that all is well. The doctor will also have to check that the abortion is complete.

She will have some bleeding like a period and she may have 'period pains' for a few days after. If the bleeding or pain is severe or if she has a raised temperature or an unusual vaginal discharge, she should see a doctor as soon as possible to check she does not have an infection or need further treatment. She will be given advice on how to reduce the risk of infection. She will also need to think about future contraception as it is possible to become pregnant as soon as 7 days after an abortion.

How do women feel after an abortion?

Most feel relief. Some women feel sadness because in other circumstances they might have welcomed a baby. Hormone levels change during pregnancy and are altered suddenly by abortion. This causes some women to feel depressed until their hormone levels get back to normal. All women find it helpful to have support from their partner, an understanding friend or a relative.

A few women feel so upset they may need to see their family doctor or a professional counsellor at an organisation specialising in this help.

Are there any long-term effects of abortion?

Having an abortion should not affect a woman's fertility (ability to have another child). She is less likely to suffer emotionally or physically than if she continued the pregnancy to full term.

• The above information is from Brook Advisory Centres. See page 41 for address details.

Religion and abortion

Information from Education for Choice

No religion actively supports abortion, but some religions accept that there are situations when abortion may be necessary.

The Roman Catholic Church is the only major world religion to rule that abortion is absolutely unacceptable in all circumstances (including the probable death of the mother). However it is only since 1869, when Pope Pius IX declared that 'ensoulment' (gaining a soul) happened at conception, that Catholics have been taught that abortion is always morally evil.

The Church of England and the Church of Scotland teach that abortion is wrong because it denies the foetus the right to life but there are certain extreme circumstances (i.e. serious risk to the health of the mother) when her needs override the rights of the foetus.

Judaism teaches that life begins at the moment of birth, however abortion is discouraged except where the mother's life is at risk. Hindu scriptures also only allow abortion under these circumstances.

Islam also teaches that abortion is permitted only in extreme circumstances in which case the actual life of the mother takes precedence over the probable life of the foetus. Some scholars also sanction abortion if the pregnancy resulted from rape. As it is believed that the foetus becomes 'ensouled' at 120 days, early abortion is preferred.

The Free Churches (Baptist, Methodist and Evangelical) hold that abortion is a matter for the individual to decide. The Methodists in particular have been outspoken in their view that personal and social factors need to be considered in each case.

However there are many people whose attitude towards abortion differs from those of their religious leaders. They believe that individuals have the right to follow their own consciences, and women from all religions continue to seek abortions.

Abortion and the Catholic Church

Definition

Abortion is the ejection of an immature and non-viable foetus from the womb. Where this happens naturally there can be no grounds for any sort of moral judgement. Where the abortion is 'procured' (done directly or caused to happen) the Church says that grave moral wrong is done.

History

From the earliest times the Church has condemned abortion. One of the earliest statements condemning abortion is in a document called the Didache, written in the 2nd century (some time after 100 A.D.): 'You shall not kill the embryo by abortion and shall not cause the newborn to perish'. The teaching has been repeated through the centuries and as early as the 4th century the Church made abortion a crime with its own proper penalties. In the 16th century, Popes Sixtus V and Gregory XIV said that causing or having an abortion means that the guilty person is automatically excommunicated (cut off from the Church). This position is clearly stated again in the Church's own collection of laws (the Code of Canon Law, 1983): 'A person who actually procures an abortion incurs automatic excommunication' (Canon 1398).

The beginning of life

The Church says that human life begins when the woman's egg is fertilised by a male sperm. From that moment a unique life begins, independent of the life of the mother and of the father. The features which distinguish us from our parents – the colour of our eyes, the shape of our face, etc. – are all laid down in the 'genetic code' that comes into existence then. Each new life that begins at this point is not a potential human being but a human being with potential. No-one can point to the twelfth day or the fourth week or any

other time and say, 'This is when I began being me.' Birth is a stage in my life and the process of life begins at conception.

The right to life

In 1980 the seven Catholic Archbishops of Great Britain (England, Wales and Scotland), issued a document called 'Abortion and the Right to Live'. The bishops take a stand against all practices that degrade human rights and dignity. It is a matter, they say, of respect for our neighbour. In their document they emphasise that the Church's opposition to abortion comes from a recognition of the basic rights of all individuals. These individuals include the unborn, who have their own intrinsic value. They also have rights which cannot be taken away from them. One such right is the right to life.

In October 1996 the Catholic Bishops of England and Wales published a pre-general election document called 'The Common Good'. In that they say that human rights all flow from the one fundamental right: the right to life (CG n. 37).

The 'Catechism of the Catholic Church' (1992) states that the embryo must be treated from conception as a person (n. 2274) and it stresses that the inalienable right to life of every innocent human individual is a constitutive element of a civil society and its legislation.

The Catechism quotes from the document 'Donum Vitae' ('The gift of life') from the Vatican's Congregation for the Doctrine of the Faith (the office that deals with matters of faith and morals). That document says:

'The inalienable rights of the person must be recognised and respected by civil society and the political authority. These human rights depend neither on single individuals nor on parents; nor do they represent a concession made by the society and the state; they belong to human nature and are inherent in the persons by virtue of the creative act from which the person took his origin. Among such fundamental rights one should mention in this regard every human being's right to life . . . from the moment of conception until death.'

In other words, I do not have a right to life because someone gives me that right; I have a right to live because I am a human being, and a human being from the moment of conception. In the same way that no-one can give me that right, no-one can take it away.

(The same arguments apply in the case of euthanasia. Nobody has the right to take away the gift of life from an old or sick person, even if that person appears to have given consent or expressed a desire to be put to death. The Church says that 'ordinary' means of preserving life should be used in the case of irreversibly or terminally ill people,

I have a right to live because I am a human being, and a human being from the moment of conception

but that 'extraordinary' means are not demanded. This is especially true when treatment may be difficult or painful and have no lasting effect. In other words, if a person is clearly soon going to die, medical care may be withdrawn and that person then be allowed to die naturally. In a case like this, it is not the carer's intention to cause the death of the patient. In all cases, treatment for pain relief should be given, since this would be classed as 'ordinary'. Food and water are not medical treament and withdrawing them from a terminally ill person is wrong and actually causes death.)

The most recent formal teaching of the pope

In 1995, Pope John Paul II wrote an encyclical letter (a teaching letter to the whole Catholic Church) called 'Evangelium Vitae' (Latin for 'The Gospel of Life'). In that he deals with three major 'life' issues, abortion, euthanasia and the destruction of human embryos in medical research. He also touches briefly on issues like suicide and the death penalty. The letter repeats very clearly the Catholic Church's position on abortion.

The basic principle is stated first: 'I confirm that the direct and voluntary killing of an innocent human being is always gravely immoral' (EV n. 57). This basic principle applies to all three cases at the heart of the letter. This principle admits that accidental and even indirect killing is not always wrong, and that legitimate self-defence can sometimes cause death.

The pope calls abortion murder, saying that we need now more than ever to have the courage to look things in the eye and call things by their proper name. He acknowledges the tragedy that abortion can often be for the mother, and the emotional suffering it might cause her. The decision is often not made for selfish reasons, but to protect things like her own health or the living standards of the rest of the family. Sometimes there is a fear that the conditions into which the child is to be born are so bad that it is better that the child is not born. Nevertheless, these reasons and others like them, however serious and tragic, can never justify the deliberate killing of an innocent human being (EV n. 58).

• The above information is from the Catholic Media Office. Visit their web site at www.catholic-ew.org.uk

Unwanted pregnancy and abortion

ALRA

THE CAMPAIGN FOR CHOICE

Could I be pregnant?

If you have had sex without using a contraceptive or the contraceptive you use has failed, you could be pregnant. Emergency contraception can prevent an unwanted pregnancy if the woman is treated within 72 hours of unprotected sex, but the sooner it is used the more likely it is to work. Pills are available from some doctors, family planning clinics or Brook Advisory Centres, or you could have an IUD (intra-uterine device) fitted.

What are the symptoms of pregnancy?

The most common sign of possible pregnancy is a missed period. Other signs are sickness, swollen breasts and passing urine more frequently

What do I do if I miss my period?

If your period is a week overdue you should go for a pregnancy test. Your doctor should be able to do this. However, if you do not want to go to your doctor, go to your local Family Planning Clinic, Brook Advisory Centre, or buy a home-test kit from a chemist. It is important that you seek help as early as possible because if you decide you do not want to continue the pregnancy and you want to seek an abortion, the earlier it is done in the pregnancy the safer it is for you. If your pregnancy test is negative but you miss another period you should have a repeat test.

If I am pregnant, what can I do?

There are three options open to you.

Firstly, if your pregnancy is unplanned, you may decide to continue with it and have a child. If this is the case, you should go to your doctor and arrange ante-natal care.

Secondly, you may decide to continue with the pregnancy and have the child adopted. Details of adoption agencies may be obtained from Citizens' Advice Bureaux, social services at your local council, local churches, The Family Planning Association, etc.

Thirdly, you may decide to seek an abortion.

Who can I talk to?

Whatever your final decision you may want to discuss all the options with someone else. This could be your doctor or a counsellor at a Family Planning Clinic or the Brook Advisory Centre. If you feel you can, you should discuss it with your parents, although you may be nervous of their reaction.

If you are under sixteen years of age and wish to seek an abortion your parents will normally need to be involved in the decision. If, however, you have strong reasons for not wanting them to know, your doctor is legally able to agree to the abortion without your parents' knowledge or consent so long as you show that you fully understand what it means to have an abortion.

What is an abortion?

An abortion is when a pregnancy is ended before a baby is capable of surviving on its own outside the mother's body. An abortion can either happen naturally, i.e. a miscarriage, or it can be induced, i.e. done deliberately. An induced abortion is only legal if it is carried out within the law and in the circumstances which the law permits.

NEVER attempt to induce an abortion yourself as this could cause you serious injury.

What does the law say about abortion?

Under the terms of the Abortion Act, a woman requires the agreement of two doctors before an abortion may be carried out. Doctors can agree to an abortion if they believe one or more of the following:

a. continuing with the pregnancy would involve more risk to your physical or mental health than terminating it.
b. continuing with the pregnancy would involve greater risk to your life than terminating it.
c. any existing children of yours would be likely to suffer if the pregnancy continued.
d. there is a substantial risk that the child would be seriously disabled.

If you are under sixteen years of age and wish to seek an abortion your parents will normally need to be involved in the decision

A doctor can take into account your financial and social circumstances when considering your request for an abortion, if you are less than 24 weeks pregnant.

Where should I go if I decide to seek an abortion?

You should first go to your doctor. If the doctor agrees to your request you would normally be referred to a local NHS hospital and seen by another doctor, who, if agreeable to the abortion, would make the arrangements for your admission to hospital.

In some cases (partly depending on where you live) NHS facilities may not be available for abortion and you may be referred to either a non-profit making clinic dealing with abortion or a private clinic. In these circumstances you may have to pay for the abortion.

What do I do if the doctor will not help me?

Some doctors do not agree with abortion, although they should refer you to another doctor. Other women for personal reasons may not wish to go to their doctor. In these circumstances you should go for help to one of the following: Family Planning Association, a Brook Advisory Centre, the British Pregnancy Advisory Service, Marie Stopes International, or a Citizens' Advice Bureau.

What does the abortion involve?

In the first nine weeks of pregnancy you may be able to take pills to bring on an abortion or in the first three months you could have a surgical operation which is a very simple procedure carried out under either local or general anaesthetic. If the abortion is carried out in a day-care unit you could be out of hospital or clinic on the same day. In other places you may have to stay overnight. If you are later into the pregnancy, the simpler abortion techniques may not be possible and you will have to stay in hospital a little longer.

How can I reduce the risks of an unwanted pregnancy?

If you are having sex and do not want a child, it is essential that you seek contraceptive advice and choose a method of contraception that suits you.

If you do not want to go to your own doctor, use your local Family Planning Clinic or Brook Advisory Centre. (Brook Advisory Centres give particular help to under 25 year olds.) REMEMBER: If the contraceptive you use fails (i.e. a burst condom) or you forget to use your contraceptive, emergency contraception used within 72 hours of unprotected sex can prevent an unwanted pregnancy.

Where can I get help?

One of the following organisations will be able to refer you to somewhere near you where you can get help:

Brook Advisory Centres (for under 25 year olds), Studio 421, Highgate Studios, 51-79 Highgate Road, London NW5 1TL. Tel: 0800 0185023

Family Planning Association, 2-12 Pentonville Road, London N1 9FP. Tel: 020 7837 4044

British Pregnancy Advisory Service,* Austy Manor, Wootton Wawen, Solihull, West Midlands B95 6BX. Tel: 08457 304030

Marie Stopes International,* 108 Whitfield Street, London W1P 6BE. Tel: 0845 300 8090

Citizens' Advice Bureau – (Address and telephone number in telephone directory).

* Provide emergency contraception for a fee.

Abortion law

Information from the British Pregnancy Advisory Service (BPAS)

The history of British abortion law

Abortion in England and Wales was first made illegal in the 19th century. Before then English Common Law had allowed abortion provided it was carried out before the woman felt the foetus move ('quickening') when it was believed the soul entered the body.

Abortions performed after quickening were an offence under Common Law but there were no fixed penalties and the woman having the abortion was not necessarily held responsible. In 1803 the law changed and abortion became a criminal offence from the time of conception with penalties of up to life imprisonment for both the pregnant woman and the abortionist.

The Offences against the Person Act 1861

Section 58 of the Offences against the Person Act 1861 made abortion a criminal offence punishable by imprisonment from three years to life, even when performed for medical reasons. No further legal changes occurred in England until 1929. The Offences against the Person Act is still in place and the current law simply provides exceptions to the 1861 law by clarifying when an abortion can be legal.

The Infant Life Preservation Act 1929

The Infant Life Preservation Act amended the law so that abortion would no longer be regarded as a felony if it was carried out in good faith for the sole purpose of preserving the life of the mother.

The 1929 Act made it illegal to kill a child 'capable of being born live', and set 28 weeks as the age at which a foetus was assumed to be able to survive.

The Infant Life Preservation Act has never applied in Scotland.

The 'Bourne Judgement' 1938

In 1938, Dr Alex Bourne performed

an abortion on a 14-year-old girl after a gang of soldiers had raped her. Dr Bourne informed the police and was prosecuted. In court, the judge ruled that Dr Bourne had acted in the 'honest belief' that the abortion would 'preserve the life of the mother'.

This opened the way for other doctors to interpret the law more flexibly because it established that preserving a woman's life could mean more than literally preventing her death.

The Abortion Act 1967

The Abortion Act 1967 came into effect on 27 April 1968 and permits termination of pregnancy subject to certain conditions. Regulations under the Act mean that abortions must be performed by a registered practitioner in a National Health Service hospital or in a location that has been specially approved by the Department of Health – such as a BPAS clinic.

An abortion may be approved providing two doctors agree in good faith that one or more of the following criteria apply:

A. the continuance of the pregnancy would involve risk to the life of the pregnant woman greater than if the pregnancy were terminated;

B. the termination is necessary to prevent grave permanent injury to the physical or mental health of the pregnant woman;

C. the continuance of the pregnancy would involve risk, greater than if the pregnancy were terminated, of injury to the physical or mental health of the pregnant woman;

D. the continuance of the pregnancy would involve risk, greater than if the pregnancy were terminated, of injury to the physical or mental health of any existing child(ren) of the family of the pregnant woman;

E. there is a substantial risk that if the child were born it would suffer from such physical or mental abnormalities as to be seriously handicapped;

or in an emergency, certified by the operating practitioner, as immediately necessary:

F. to save the life of the pregnant woman; or

G. to prevent grave permanent injury to the physical or mental health of the pregnant woman.

In relation to grounds C and D the doctor may take account of the pregnant woman's actual or reasonably foreseeable environment, including her social and economic circumstances.

Most abortions of unwanted pregnancies are carried out under grounds C or D because the doctor confirms that it would be damaging to the woman's mental health to force her to continue the pregnancy.

Doctors and other medical staff have the legal right to 'conscientiously object' to taking part in abortions unless this is necessary to save the life or prevent grave permanent injury to the woman.

Human Fertilisation and Embryology Act 1990

Section 37 of the Human Fertilisation and Embryology Act made changes to the Abortion Act. It introduced a time limit of 24 weeks for grounds C and D. Grounds A, B and E are now without limit. Before this change a 28-week limit had applied for all grounds.

The Human Fertilisation and Embryology Act also confirmed that when a woman had a multiple pregnancy it was legal for a doctor to terminate the life of one or more foetuses leaving others alive.

The Abortion Act 1967 and Section 37 of the Human Fertilisation and Embryology Act 1990 do not apply to Northern Ireland.

We welcome your views on our service. If you have a comment to make please contact the British Pregnancy Advisory Service.

• The above information is from the British Pregnancy Advisory Service (BPAS). See page 41 for address details.

Abortion methods

Information from the British Pregnancy Advisory Service (BPAS)

What an abortion involves

Abortion procedures change according to the gestation (stage) of the pregnancy. The gestation is measured in weeks counting from the first day of the woman's last menstrual period.

Up to 9 weeks

Early medical abortion

This method is also known as the abortion pill but this is not a very accurate description, as it does not involve simply taking a pill. During an early medical abortion, drugs are used to cause an early miscarriage. One works by blocking the action of the hormone that makes the lining of the uterus (womb) hold onto the fertilised egg. The other, given 48 hours later, causes the uterus to cramp. The lining of the uterus breaks down and the embryo is lost in the bleeding that follows, as happens with a miscarriage.

5 to 15 weeks

Vacuum aspiration abortion

Vacuum aspiration simply means suction. During a vacuum aspiration abortion a thin, round-ended plastic tube is eased into the uterus through the cervix, the passage that links the vagina to the womb. The contents of the uterus pass into the tube using a gentle pump.

It is possible to have a vacuum aspiration abortion under local anaesthetic or general anaesthetic.

15 to 19 weeks

Surgical dilatation and evacuation (D&E)

After the woman has been given a light general anaesthetic, the doctor gently stretches the passage through the cervix until it is wide enough for narrow forceps to be used to remove most of the contents of the uterus.

Then a tube attached to a vacuum pump is used to remove any remaining tissue.

20 to 24 weeks

Surgical two-stage abortion or medical induction

During a medical induction, the foetal heart is stopped and then the doctor uses drugs to induce premature labour.

A surgical two-stage abortion involves one procedure to cut the umbilical cord and another surgical procedure to remove the contents of the womb. The woman is given a general anaesthetic before each stage.

How does abortion affect women?

Legal abortion is a relatively safe procedure particularly when experienced doctors provide it. However, no clinical procedures are completely free from risk.

Abortion is less risky to a woman's health than continuing a pregnancy and having a baby, especially when provided in the first 12 weeks. Serious physical problems during the abortion are rare and only occur in one or two out of every thousand abortions.

Minor complications are a little more common.

Sometimes the abortion may need to be repeated because fragments of the pregnancy remain in the uterus. This occurs in around one per cent of cases.

About 10 per cent of women consult a doctor about pain or bleeding in the first month after an abortion but mostly these women simply need reassurance. One or two out of every hundred women who have abortions have an infection and are treated with antibiotics.

Overall, studies of the long-term physical effects of abortion based on groups of up to several thousand women show that abortion does not affect subsequent pregnancies or reduce fertility. Some of the one or two women in every 1000 women who have a serious abortion complication may experience reduced fertility or may be unable to conceive again.

Several studies have shown that having an abortion does not lead to psychological problems. Although women may regret having to have an abortion the vast majority find that they have no emotional problems after it. A small number – about three per cent – have long-term feelings of guilt and some of these feel that the abortion was a mistake. But for these women the unwanted pregnancy was usually one of many problems in their lives, and these problems continued after the abortion. There is some evidence that for most of these women not having the abortion would have made matters worse.

Many women feel relieved once it is over and, looking back, view the decision to end the pregnancy as regrettable but necessary.

Many women feel relieved once it is over and, looking back, view the decision to end the pregnancy as regrettable but necessary

Men and abortion

If your partner is unexpectedly pregnant, please sit down and read this. It contains information that could be important to the health and future of both of you.

Talking with your partner

Men and women communicate in very different ways. Women place a lot of emphasis on first impressions and in this situation even a neutral reaction may be seen as a lack of support. One woman said she had an abortion because her partner's first reaction was, 'Okay, I don't mind either way'. Another because her partner casually said, 'If you want', and changed the subject. Both women took this casualness to be a lack of interest and support, but found out later that all their partners needed was time to adjust to the new situation. If you really want to help your partner you should talk openly and frankly, get as much information as possible and don't base your decision on the results of one conversation. Above all ask your partner to give you time to think things through.

You may feel that because of the way society has labelled abortion as a 'woman's issue', that your partner's decision has nothing to do with you. You may think that your partner should be taking this decision on her own. But is this true?

With many couples the responsibility for an abortion decision also rests with the man because few women will have an abortion against the wishes of a supportive partner. Her response will depend on how you react. What your partner needs to know is what you truly think. Saying 'whatever you want' still leaves the weight on her shoulders.

Your partner needs reassurance that you are not planning to abandon her. That you care enough to face with her the consequences of your sexual relationship.

Effects of abortion

Generally men know very little about abortion. Abortion is not something to be considered lightly – there are physical and mental health risks to abortion.

Trauma from an abortion can also affect men. Guilt and hurt after an abortion can drive couples apart, especially if one partner was unsure about the decision. Often couples split up following an abortion.

You may want your relationship back to where it used to be, but this is impossible. Sometimes men react with a gut instinct that it is better to do something quickly and worry about the consequences later. A common reaction is 'get rid of it'. But this is not one of those situations, and an abortion will not put things back as they were. In short, both you and your partner have been permanently changed by the pregnancy.

Some men feel guilty about what they have done and then find it difficult to form close relationships in the future. Some disguise their feelings by remaining emotionally cold and distant. One man said, 'following the abortion I split up with my girlfriend and it was only years later I realised that I had never settled down and got married because of the abortion'.

There is a deep instinct in men to protect women and children. An abortion can undermine a man's confidence in himself and he can come to think of himself as a failure – a failure as a partner, a failure as a father, a failure as a man.

Many men's lives have been harmed by abortion. That is why it is important that you are involved in the decision, allow yourself plenty of time to think things through and talk openly with your partner.

Making your decision

If you really want to help your partner be honest with her. This is a tough and confusing situation. But it can also be a chance to change and mature. Are you going to run? Or will you take the first steps of genuine love by staying with her when the going gets tough? In either case, your partner is not the only one who has to make some important choices.

If you need help

If you would like to talk confidentially and privately to one of our counsellors, either with your partner or on your own, please give us a call at the number below and arrange an appointment at the centre.

The counsellor will help you work through to a considered decision on how to tackle this crisis. If you prefer we can even arrange for you to discuss the situation with a man. You will be offered complete information including understanding the alternatives to abortion. You will have space and time to think so that your decision is neither hurried nor based on ignorance.

We hope that this will help you to reach the right decision for your life.

If you would like to be put in touch with a counsellor in your area, please telephone 01256 477300

Abortion: an introduction

Information from Education for Choice

Every day a million women around the world find out that they're pregnant. Half of these women get pregnant without meaning or wanting to. As a result around one quarter of all pregnancies ends in abortion.

Education for Choice provides information about unwanted pregnancy and abortion from a pro-choice perspective. We begin with the standpoint that abortion is morally and medically acceptable. We believe a woman faced with an unwanted pregnancy should have the right to choose an abortion if that is what she decides is the best solution for her.

What is an abortion?

When people talk about abortion they usually mean the deliberate ending of a pregnancy. The deliberate removal of the foetus from the womb is called a termination of pregnancy, although the medical term for this procedure is 'induced abortion'. A foetus can be lost from the womb for natural reasons and this is often called miscarriage, although the medical term for this situation is 'spontaneous abortion'.

Why women choose abortion

There are many reasons why women choose to have an abortion instead of carrying on with an unwanted pregnancy. Here are some of them:

- They are too young or too old.
- It's the wrong time in their lives.
- They are single and lack support.
- Their baby is likely to be born seriously disabled.
- They have no home or secure base.
- They are pregnant as a result of rape or incest.
- They have a serious disease which would be made worse by the pregnancy.
- They have relationship or marriage problems.

EDUCATION FOR CHOICE
- providing educational resources on abortion

Arguments for and against abortion

The subject of abortion arouses fierce debate.

Anti-abortionists describe abortion as murder because they believe that a fertilised egg is a human being which possesses a soul from the moment of conception. They claim that it has the right to life under all circumstances.

Pro-choice supporters see the fertilised egg as a potential life. This view is based on medical and scientific evidence that the foetus is not viable – that means that it is not capable of independent life – in the early stages of pregnancy and that it is still a part of the woman until that time.

Artificially induced abortion is therefore legally and morally acceptable until about 24 weeks. A small number of abortions each year do take place after 24 weeks in cases where the foetus would not survive, or is likely to be born severely disabled, or the life or health of the woman is in danger.

Pro-choice supporters believe that people should be allowed to make their own decisions about abortion according to their own moral beliefs.

• The above information is from Education for Choice. See page 41 for their address details.

What people think about abortion

At the moment, the law requires the permission of two doctors for an abortion; it is not ultimately the woman's decision. A Harris poll published in April 1998 asked the question:

'Should a pregnant woman be able to decide for herself whether to have an abortion in the first 3 months of pregnancy?'

A sample of 1762 adults in Britain were interviewed face-to-face.
77% said yes;
12% said no;
11% didn't know.
Slightly more women than men agreed: 81% of women and 72% of men.

People in the age groups most likely to have children agreed more readily than the youngest or oldest groups:

Age	%
Age 16-17:	73%;
18-24:	71%;
25-34:	81%;
35-44:	80%;
45-54:	78%;
55-64:	77%;
65+:	73%.

Opinion polls are a way of finding out what people think about major issues. Many people find it difficult to talk openly with friends and family about abortion and the lack of public debate can mean that law-makers are not aware of the views held by the majority of the people they were elected to serve. Used responsibly, public opinion polls can point the way to change.

Opinions on abortion

Information from British Pregnancy Advisory Service (BPAS)

Arguments for and against abortion

People often have strong views about abortion. These are some of the arguments used to justify legal abortion, or to oppose it.

The arguments against legal abortion

- Human life begins at conception and abortion destroys respect for human life.
- Abortion is a violent act that damages a mother and her baby. It is uncivilised and unjust.
- There are alternatives to abortion, such as adoption.
- Abortion damages women because they suffer post-abortion guilt and trauma.
- Abortion is rarely necessary to save the life of the woman.
- Abortion encourages brutality towards children and child-abuse.
- Abortion on grounds of foetal abnormality encourages discrimination against disabled people.

The arguments for legal abortion

- The embryo or foetus should be respected as potential human life but does not have the same value as a born person.
- Women are capable of making the right moral choices and can follow their own consciences.
- A pregnant woman understands her own personal circumstances better than anyone else and so is in the best position to know whether she should or should not have a child.
- Legal abortion is relatively safe and is likely to cause a woman less harm than forcing her to continue her pregnancy and have an unwanted child.
- It is better for children to be born to parents who want and love them.
- It is not possible to prevent unwanted pregnancies by contraception alone.

- Public opinion supports legal abortion.
- When abortion is illegal women tend to travel elsewhere because they are so desperate to avoid having to continue an unwanted pregnancy.

What is the alternative?

There is no practical alternative to easily accessible legal abortion. If the law denied abortion to women with unplanned pregnancies then they would either travel to places where they could obtain abortions or they would seek illegal procedures in this country as they did before 1967.

Some women, possibly tens of thousands each year, would become mothers of unplanned, unwanted children. This would have major consequences for individual women, for public health and for society as a whole. Therefore it is not in the interests of individual women or society to turn the clock back.

Public opinion on abortion

Public opinion in Great Britain and Northern Ireland supports legal abortion.

A MORI poll commissioned in February 1997 by BPAS and Birth Control Trust showed that 64 per cent of those asked agreed with the statement 'Abortion should be made legally available for all who want it', while 25 per cent disagreed. The proportion of British adults who agreed with the statement had increased by 10 per cent since 1980, while the proportion that disagreed had fallen by 11 per cent.

Public opinion in Britain supports legal abortion. Only a small minority opposes abortion in all circumstances. Polls suggest that most people support a more liberal abortion law.

Religious positions on abortion

Roman Catholic

The Roman Catholic Church holds the view that life begins at the moment of conception and should be protected from this time. In 1869 Pope Pius IX declared that ensoulment takes place at conception and since then this has been restated frequently in documents expressing the official church teaching.

Church of England
The Church of England holds the view that all human life is created by God and should be nurtured, supported and protected. This principle applies to both the mother and the foetus therefore the Church recognises the need for a balance between compassion for the mother and responsibility for the life of the foetus. In 1983 the General Synod passed a resolution that recognised that 'in situations where the continuance of the pregnancy threatens the life of the mother, a termination of pregnancy may be justified and that there must be adequate and safe provision in our society for such situations'.

Church of Scotland
In 1988 the Church of Scotland Board of Social Responsibility recommended that abortion be permitted 'on grounds that the continuance of the pregnancy would involve serious risk to the life or present great danger to the health, whether physical or mental, of the pregnant woman'.

Jewish
Judaism permits abortion if the mother's life is at risk through continuing the pregnancy, which includes the risk of suicide.

Muslim
Islam holds the view that abortion is permitted in extreme circumstances such as when the mother's life is endangered. Some Islamic scholars would also sanction abortion if the pregnancy was the result of rape.

Abortion is seen as more acceptable if it takes place before 120 days when it is believed the soul enters the foetus.

Hindu
Hinduism traditionally forbids abortion except for serious medical reasons.

Buddhism
Buddhists are free to act according to their own insights and understanding, at the same time Buddhism teaches that people should act responsibly. They undertake to cultivate an attitude of loving kindness (metta) and compassion (karuna) to living things.

Abortion can be a responsible choice. It has no fewer morals than the decision to have a child

Humanism
Humanism is not a religion but a system of ethical beliefs based on the view that humans should take responsibility for their own lives and show concern for the quality of life of others. Tolerance and open-mindedness are valued. Humanists believe that human life should be valued but do not believe that there is a clear point at which a foetus becomes a person. Humanists believe that there are no moral grounds for refusing an abortion in early pregnancy and even in late pregnancy abortion may be 'the humane and moral choice'.

Official church teaching on abortion does not necessarily influence the decisions women make. It is common for Catholics to disagree with church teaching on abortion and abortion is common in many Catholic countries.

What does BPAS believe about abortion?

BPAS believes that abortion should be legal and that women should be free to decide if, and when, they have children.

Those who oppose abortion are a minority. They are entitled to their views and values but they should respect the views and values of others.

Better sex education and improved contraceptive services would help women avoid unwanted pregnancy but would not eliminate the need for abortion entirely. Contraception is not 100% effective and a planned pregnancy may become a problem.

Abortion is an essential part of health care and should be freely available through a publicly funded NHS.

Abortion can be a responsible choice. It has no fewer morals than the decision to have a child.

• BPAS supports reproductive choice by advocating and providing high-quality affordable services to prevent or end unwanted pregnancy with contraception or by abortion. See page 41 for their address details.

Opinions on abortion

Abortion should be made legally available for all that want it

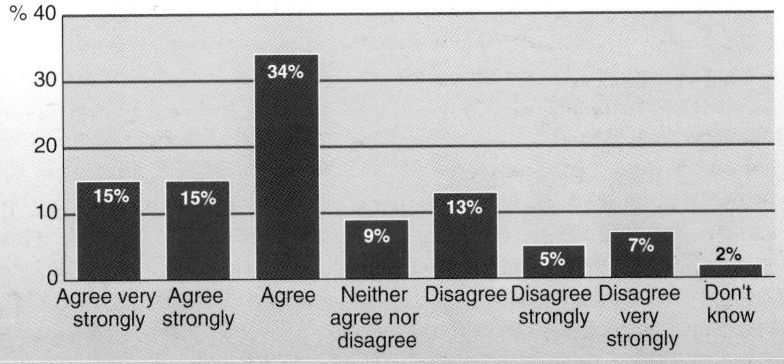

Response	%
Agree very strongly	15%
Agree strongly	15%
Agree	34%
Neither agree nor disagree	9%
Disagree	13%
Disagree strongly	5%
Disagree very strongly	7%
Don't know	2%

Circumstances when people approve or disapprove of abortion

	Approve	Disapprove	Don't know
When the woman's life is in danger	93%	3%	4%
When the woman's health is at risk	88%	6%	6%
In a case of rape	88%	6%	6%
When the child would have a mental disability	67%	20%	13%
When the child would have a physical disability	66%	21%	13%
When the woman was under 16	58%	29%	13%

Source: BPAS

Ethical consideration of abortion

Information from the British Medical Association (BMA)

Moral arguments

People generally take one of three main stances on abortion: pro-abortion, anti-abortion and the middle ground that abortion is acceptable in some circumstances. The main arguments for each of these positions are set out below.

Arguments used in support of abortion

Those who support the wide availability of abortion consider that abortion is not wrong in itself and need not involve undesirable consequences. These arguments tend not to recognise foetal rights or to acknowledge the foetus to be a person. According to some, abortion is a matter of a woman's right to exercise control over her own body. Moralists who judge actions by their consequences alone could argue that abortion is equivalent to a deliberate failure to conceive a child and since contraception is widely available, abortion should be too. Some think that even if the foetus is a person, its rights are very limited and do not weigh significantly against the interests of people who have already been born, such as parents or existing children of the family. The interests of society at large might outweigh any right accorded to the foetus in some circumstances, such as if, for example, overpopulation or famine threatened that society. In such cases, abortion might be seen by some people as moving from a neutral act to one which should be encouraged. Similarly utilitarians who see a duty to promote the greatest happiness and maximise the number of worthwhile lives, could argue that there should be as few as possible unwanted children in the world.

Most people who support this position do so on the basis that the overriding principle is the woman's right to choose what happens to her body. This use of the language of 'choice' conveys approval regardless of the type of pressures the individual faces and any constraints on her freedom to make a genuine choice.

Arguments used against abortion

Some people consider that abortion is wrong in any circumstances because it fails to recognise the rights of the foetus or because it challenges the notion of the sanctity of all human life. Some argue that permitting abortion diminishes the respect society feels for other vulnerable humans, possibly leading to their involuntary euthanasia. Those who consider that an embryo, from the moment of conception, is a human being with full moral status, see abortion as killing in the same sense as the murder of any other person. Those who take this view cannot accept that women should be allowed to obtain abortion without legal repercussions, however difficult the lives of those women or their existing families are made as a result.

Such views may be based on religious or moral convictions that each human life has unassailable intrinsic value, which is not diminished by any impairment or suffering that may be involved for the individual living that life. It is also argued that abortion treats humans merely as a means to an end in that abortion can be seen as a discarding of a foetus in which the pregnant woman no longer has any interest. Many worry that the availability of abortion on grounds of foetal abnormality encourages prejudice towards any person with a handicap and insidiously creates the impression that the only valuable people are those who conform to some ill-defined stereotype of 'normality'.

Some people who oppose abortion in general, concede that it may be justifiable in very exceptional cases such as where it is the result of rape or the consequence of exploitation of a young girl or a mentally incompetent woman. Risk to the mother's life may be another justifiable exception but only where abortion is the only option. It would thus not be seen as justifiable to abort a foetus if the life of both foetus and mother could be saved by any other solution.

Arguments used to support abortion in some circumstances

Many people argue that abortion may be justified in a greater number of circumstances than those conceded by anti-abortionists but that it would be undesirable to allow abortion on demand. To do so might incur undesirable effects, such as encouraging irresponsible attitudes to contraception. It could also lead to a devaluation of the lives of viable foetuses and trivialise the potential psychological effects of abortion on women and on health professionals.

These types of argument are based on the premise that the embryo starts off without rights, although having a special status from conception in view of its potential for development, and that it acquires rights and status throughout its development. The notion of developing foetal rights and practical factors, such as the possible distress to the pregnant woman, nurses, doctors or other children in the family, gives rise to the view that early abortion is more acceptable than late abortion.

Some people support this position on pragmatic grounds, believing that abortions will always be sought by women who are desperate and that it is better for society to provide abortion services which are safe and which can be monitored and regulated, rather than to allow 'back-street' practices.

The BMA's view on abortion

In the 1970s and 1980s the BMA approved policy statements supporting the 1967 Abortion Act as 'a practical and humane piece of legislation' and calling for its expansion to Northern Ireland. The BMA does not consider that abortion is unethical but as with any act having profound moral implications, the justifications must be commensurate with the consequences. The BMA's advice to its members is to act within the boundaries of the law and of their own conscience. Patients are, however, entitled to receive objective medical advice regardless of their doctor's personal views for or against abortion. Furthermore, a doctor could be sued for damages if, because of a failure to refer, a delay is caused which results in the woman being unable to obtain a termination.

- Requests for advice or further information should be directed to: Medical Ethics Department, British Medical Association, BMA House, Tavistock Square, London WC1H 9JP

Matters of death or life

'We favour terminating pregnancy at 9 months – not killing children' (Feminists for Life)

Did you know?

- 97% of abortions are performed on healthy babies
- Abortion is available up to 24 weeks (premature babies have survived at 22 weeks) and up to birth if the baby is disabled (harelip is sufficient disability)
- Recent statistics show abortion figures have increased by 14%
- Nearly 200,000 abortions are performed in England, Scotland and Wales each year
- Roughly 42% of all baby girls are aborted, against only 25% of baby boys (Planned Parenthood data). In Bombay out of 7,999 abortions performed only one baby was male (WHO Report)
- Founder members of the pro-abortion lobby were well-known eugenicists.
- Founder members of the Feminist Movement were opposed to abortion. Mary Wollstonecraft decried the sexual exploitation of women which caused them to either 'destroy the embryo in the womb, or cast it off when born. Nature in everything demands respect.' A *Vindication of the Rights of Women*
- While 245,000 American women who had had abortions joined the National Right to Life, only 39,000 women joined the National Abortion League
- Physical complications of legal abortion include cervical injury, 200% increased risk of miscarriage after two or more abortions, 160% increased risk of tubal pregnancy, increased risk of breast cancer, decrease in fertility
- No one knows the true extent of backstreet abortion before 1967, but total female death rates from 1951 onwards have shown little variation. Sad stories of backstreet abortions are taken from the thirties, not the fifties. Better antibiotics have had more influence on women's health than the legalisation of abortion. Nevertheless there has been a significant increase in the complications resulting from abortion, simply because there have been so many more abortions since 1967
- Doctors in India have transplanted light-sensitive cells from the eyes of 14-19-week-old healthy aborted foetuses into the eyes of blind adults suffering from Retinitis Pigmentosa
- Healthy foetal tissue is used in experimental treatment for Parkinson's, Huntington's and Alzheimer's disease.

Abortion

Information from Education for Choice

Background

Abortion has been used throughout the world for thousands of years.

In the UK abortion became illegal in the 19th century when the penalty for 'procuring a miscarriage' was life imprisonment. Women trying to escape the burden of an unwanted pregnancy were forced to use unreliable and dangerous methods, including poisonous drugs, knitting needles, soap or lead solutions inserted through syringes, and blows to the abdomen.

However many people were appalled by the number of women suffering and dying as a result of illegal abortion. Pressure for reform finally resulted in Liberal MP David Steel's Abortion Law Reform Bill, which became law on 27 October 1967 and took effect on 27 April 1968.

This was amended in 1990 by the Human Fertilisation and Embryology Act which changed the upper limit from 28 to 24 weeks for most abortions, due to the fact that advances in medicine mean it is now possible to keep some babies alive born after about 24 weeks of pregnancy.

Since 1967, there have been over 20 unsuccessful attempts in Parliament to restrict the law, prompted by pressure groups opposed to legal abortion. However, recent polls show more than 80% of adults are in favour of abortion on request.

Ethics

The subject of abortion arouses fierce debate. People who are against abortion describe it as murder because they believe that a fertilised egg is a human being which possesses a soul from the moment of conception, and has the right to life under all circumstances. Pro-choice supporters see the fertilised egg as potential life, based on medical and scientific evidence that the foetus is not viable (i.e. capable of independent life) in the early stages of pregnancy and is still a part of its mother. In fact nature chooses not to allow all fertilised eggs to develop: it is estimated that as many as 25% of pregnancies end in spontaneous abortion or miscarriage.

Abortion has existed throughout history and making it illegal or socially unacceptable does not drive it away – it merely adds to the pain and danger which women are prepared to face to avoid carrying on with an unwanted pregnancy. People who have a moral or religious objection to abortion should not be forced to have or to participate in an abortion against their will. Should they be allowed to use the law to impose their views on those who do not share their beliefs?

Abortion has existed throughout history and making it illegal or socially unacceptable does not drive it away

If women are to enjoy a healthy, happy life and to offer the same to any children they may have, they need to be able to exercise control over their reproductive lives. Not all women are able to use contraception effectively at all times. Surely a request for an abortion is a responsible decision when faced with the prospect of a child that she is not able to love or care for? Why should a woman seeking abortion be accused of having no respect for life when her prime concern has been the future quality of life for herself, the potential child, her partner and her family?

Although it is women whose health and well-being are most affected by the availability of abortion, it is often men who have the power to decide. That is why pro-choice groups continue to press for a woman's right to decide for herself, believing that society should recognise that women are trustworthy, responsible people who are capable of making valid judgements for themselves on moral issues.

• The above is an excerpt from *Abortion – an overview*, produced by Education for Choice and available on their web site which can be found at www.efc.org.uk Alternatively, see page 41 for their address details.

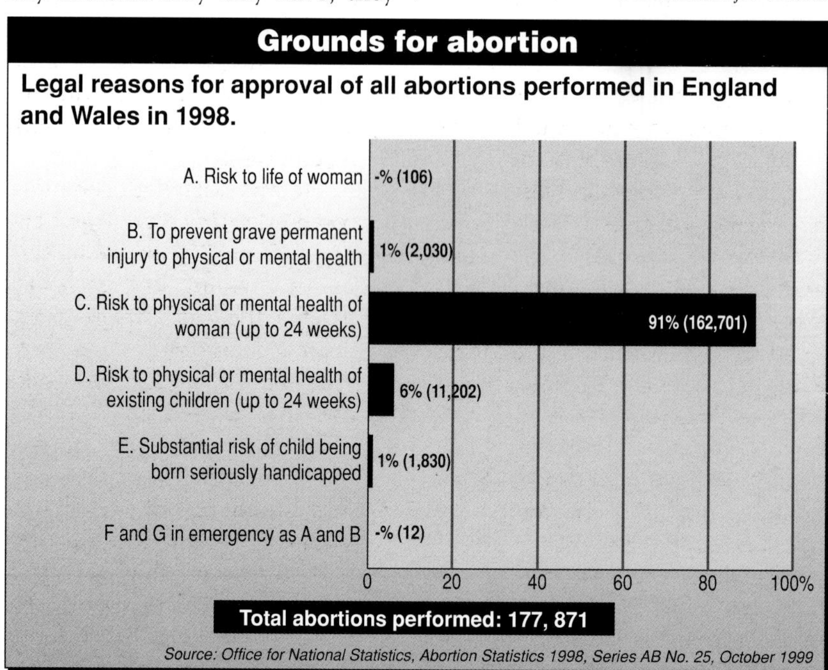

A non-religious perspective on abortion

Information from the British Humanist Association (BHA)

Abortion is a subject that demonstrates the difficulties of rigid rules in moral decision making. Medical science has advanced to the point where we have options that were unthinkable even a few generations ago and where old rules cannot cope with new facts.

Some medical facts

- Some very premature babies can now be kept alive, which has altered ideas about when foetuses become human beings with human rights.
- Many illnesses and disabilities can now be diagnosed long before birth.
- Some very ill or disabled babies who would probably once have died before or shortly after birth can now be kept alive.
- The sex of a foetus can be known well before birth (and some parents would like to be able to choose the sex of their child).
- Genetic research makes it increasingly likely that parents will be able to know, or even to choose, other characteristics for their unborn child. A few will want to reject some foetuses.
- Abortions can be performed safely, though they can occasionally cause medical or psychological problems.

These are in themselves morally neutral medical facts, but they bring with them the necessity to make moral choices and to consider who should make those choices. Doctors? Politicians? Religious leaders? Medical ethics committees? Individual women? Their partners?

Some views on abortion

Some examples of contemporary rules and views about abortion will perhaps demonstrate the complexity of the problem:

- Some religious people think that all human life is sacred, that life begins at conception, and so abortion is always wrong (and some also believe that contraception is wrong, which leads to even more unwanted pregnancies). But if one has to choose between risking the life of the mother or the life of the unborn foetus, how does one decide whose life is more 'sacred'? (This is very rare these days, and the choice is most often about the quality of life of either the mother or the foetus or both.)
- People often argue that it is not for doctors 'to play God' and that it is for God to decide matters of life and death. But it could be said that all medical interventions are 'playing God' (even your childhood vaccinations may have kept you alive longer than 'God' planned) so we have to decide for ourselves how we use medical powers. Arguments which invoke God are unconvincing to those who do not believe in gods, and laws should not be based on claims which rely on religious faith.
- Some moral philosophers have argued that full consciousness begins only after birth or even later, and so foetuses and infants are not full human beings with human rights.
- Doctors have a range of opinions on abortion, but tend to give the medical interests of the mother (which may include her mental health) the most weight when making decisions.
- Some doctors and nurses dislike carrying out abortions because they feel that their job is to save life, not to destroy it.
- Some people believe that a woman has absolute rights over her own body which override those of any unborn foetus. You might like to read Judith Jarvis Thomson's *A Defense of Abortion* which states a feminist case for abortion very clearly.
- The law in England, Scotland and Wales is based on the fact that after twenty-four weeks the foetus is often viable, in that with medical care it can survive outside the womb.
- The law in England, Scotland and Wales states that an abortion can be performed before the twenty-fourth week of pregnancy if two doctors agree that there is a risk to the life or the mental or physical health of the mother if the pregnancy continues, or there will be a risk to the mental or physical health of other children in the family. However, there is no time limit if there is a substantial risk that the baby will be born severely disabled, or there is a grave risk of death or permanent injury (mental or physical) to the mother. In effect this means that almost every woman who wants an abortion and is persistent in seeking one before the twenty-fourth week can obtain one. However, some women who do not realise that they are pregnant till too late (perhaps because they are very young or because they are menopausal) may not be able to have abortions though they would have qualified on other grounds.

The humanist view

So how do humanists pick their way between these conflicting ideas? Humanists respect life and value happiness and personal choice, so they might agree with many of the above points. And in a democratic nation such as the UK, they would respect and obey the law, though they recognise that the law is not always the same as justice or morality, and would campaign for changes when they consider laws to be unjust.

In any case, the current law is simply permissive; it does not impose abortion on anyone who does not want it, so even within the law, people have to make moral choices.

Because humanists take happiness and suffering into consideration, they are more concerned with the quality of life than the right to life, if the two come into conflict. The probable quality of life of the baby, the woman, the father and the rest of the family, the doctors and nurses involved, would all have to be given due weight. There is plenty of room for debate about how much weight each individual should have, but most humanists would probably put the interests of the woman first, since she would have to complete the pregnancy and probably care for the baby, whose happiness would largely depend on hers. She also exists already with other responsibilities and rights and desires which can be taken into account – unlike those of the unborn foetus which cannot be so surely ascertained.

Of course all possible options should be explored and decisions should be informed ones. Adoption of the unwanted baby might be a better solution in some cases. On reflection a woman might decide that she could look after a sick or disabled child. Or she might decide that she cannot offer this child a life worth living and abortion is the better choice. She will need to consider the long-term effects as well as the immediate ones. It is unlikely to be an easy decision, and requiring an abortion is a situation that most women would prefer to avoid.

For society as a whole, as well as for the children themselves, the existence of unwanted children cannot be a good thing, and this is doubtless the rationale behind the current law. However, abortion is not the best way of avoiding unwanted children, and improved sex education, easily available contraception, and better education and opportunities for young women, can all help to reduce the number of abortions. But as long as abortion is needed as a last resort, most humanists would agree that society should provide safe legal facilities. The alternatives, which would inevitably include illegal abortions, are far worse.

Some further questions to consider

- Is abortion in the case of conception after rape more justified than other abortions?
- Would a humanist favour abortion if a woman wanted one because her pregnancy was interfering with her holiday plans? Why (not)?
- Why do humanists think contraception is better than abortion?
- Are there any good arguments against adoption of unwanted babies?
- Should doctors and nurses impose their moral views on patients? Yes? Sometimes? Never?
- Should religious people impose their views on abortion on non-religious people? Yes? Sometimes? Never?
- Should parents be able to choose the sex of their child? Should they be able to abort a foetus of the 'wrong' sex?
- At what point does a foetus become a human being? Does it make any difference to the humanist view of abortion?
- Can infanticide ever be right?
- Should abortion ever be carried out on a non-consenting woman, e.g. one too young to give legal consent or one in a coma?
- How are you deciding your answers to these questions?

A woman's right to choose?

Information from LIFE

We all know what abortion does to the unborn child. But there's one other very important person involved. The woman. What happens to her?

What we are told

For over 25 years women in Britain have been told that abortion was a safe little procedure, involving no big problems. Women needed abortion to have total control over their fertility and total freedom to choose what to do with their lives. Abortion would bring with it a new status for women. At last women would be equal with men because they would not have to bear unwanted children. So were are told.

Safe little procedure?

Abortion is invasive of women's bodies whatever method is used, whether surgical or chemical. Surgical methods can damage future fertility as well as cause immediate infection. Chemical abortion uses drugs that are immediately dangerous for some women, painful to use, and can have still-uncharted long-term effects on women's health.

After abortion women are more likely to miscarry or give birth prematurely.

No big problems?

Abortion causes more than physical damage to women. Abortion abuses women. It leaves many women filled with anger, guilt, regret, loss of self-esteem, and unable to trust others. Relationships often collapse after abortion, and many women are left with no man, no baby, and alienated parents. No one forgets an abortion.

For some women the strain of coping, often alone, with their feelings afterwards causes more problems than any posed by the unwanted pregnancy.

Total control over their fertility?

The amount of unplanned pregnancy has risen steadily since abortion was legalised. This is despite free contraception for everyone, even under-age girls, since 1974. So what's happened to fertility control?

Readily available abortion means that, if conception occurs, the problem can be 'solved' at once. Inevitably there is more sexual activity at ever younger ages. No contraception, much of which is anyway abortifacient, is totally effective. So there are more and more unplanned pregnancies.

Freedom to choose?

When pregnancy is unwanted what real choice is there?

The choice is between abortion, with its physical and emotional after-effects, or continuing the pregnancy. Those people closely involved with the pregnant woman know that if pregnancy continues they will be expected to do something to help her and her baby. If she has an abortion they need do nothing. She has the abortion alone. She has to live with it afterwards – alone.

For selfish partners, parents, friends, the choice is simple. They do the choosing, not her. Sometimes the pressure is gentle. Often it isn't. there is little freedom of choice when those who should give love and support walk away leaving her to cope alone. Readily available abortion has made women more vulnerable.

Control over their lives?

Pregnancy changes a woman's life, whether or not it ends in abortion. It is possible to plan ahead when continuing pregnancy, and the problems and joys of motherhood can be foreseen. But abortion is a journey into the unknown. No one knows what she will feel like afterwards, either immediately or in the future. Many women are unprepared for the destructive effects of abortion on their lives.

Status of women

But, say the abortionists, it's necessary for the equal status of women that there is safe legal abortion. Unless women can enjoy the same access to hassle-free sex that men, allegedly, have traditionally enjoyed for centuries, they will never be equal, never have the same chances as men.

Well, in Great Britain women have had 25 years of this chance of achieving equal status. What's happened?

A third of births are now to women who are not married. That may include women in a stable relationship who choose not to marry and have the full support of their partner in childrearing. But it undoubtedly includes many lone mothers who chose against abortion and find they have to cope alone.

Instead of the women enjoying the sexual freedom allegedly conferred by abortion it seems to be exactly what uncaring men like. If the man doesn't want to be involved he just says, 'It's your choice', and pushes off. Some women will then have an abortion but many won't because they know what abortion can do to them, and they appreciate the rights of the child.

A new underclass

These brave women often find that, apart from LIFE, not a lot of people are interested in helping them. The new poor in Britain include many lone mothers with young babies. Are they liberated? Is their status as mothers, as women, appreciated? No. Instead, they are criticised by Government and media pundits as a burden on society.

The enormous rise in divorce has damaged the status of many women. No one asks what the connection is between abortion and divorce. Why not? If most unmarried relationships break up after abortion, won't abortion also damage marriage? One-third of women having abortions are married. One-third of marriages end in divorce in Britain. Are the two facts connected?

New role-models

The status of women in their unique role as mothers and homemakers has never been so low. All the skills women were traditionally praised for and proud of – connected with family care and home-making – are officially rubbished by the abortion-driven propagandists. Female role-models we are invited to admire usually include women who support abortion, reject children or cannot sustain a relationship.

And where is the enhanced status of women in the visual arts, media, literature? There has never been more violence and pornography directed at and involving women – as well as children. What is the connection between abortion and

One-third of women having abortions are married. One-third of marriages end in divorce in Britain. Are the two facts connected?

the way in which women are routinely portrayed even on prime-time television – the rapes, the beatings, the foul language, the sheer vulgarity?

Violence

Abortion itself violates women. And the message that violence is acceptable to women has bred dangerously.

Easy abortion makes women's bodies finally available for sex, with (apparently) no fear of the consequences, and the approval of the chattering classes. So what's wrong in taking the violence and disposability ever further?

The truly pro-woman way

LIFE has for over 20 years counselled and helped hundreds of thousands of women and their families with the problems caused by unwanted pregnancy and abortion. Most members of LIFE are women, with extensive experience of the fears, wishes, hopes of women. LIFE knows that abortion 'solves' nothing, usually leaves women in the same difficult situation as before, and often does such damage to the health of women that they are worse off than ever.

LIFE's free, confidential care for women provides a better way forward in even the most difficult situation: even when pregnancy results from rape, incest or abuse, or the unborn child has been diagnosed as disabled.

LIFE gives help that accepts and respects women and their babies.

LIFE's is the truly pro-woman way.

8 myths about abortion

Information from the National Abortion Campaign (NAC)

Abortion only happens to other people
Four out of ten women have had or will have an abortion at some time in this country, according to government statistics.

Abortion is available on demand
You need the permission of two doctors before you can have an abortion, unlike most countries in Europe where it is available on request.

Abortion is dangerous
You are over seven times more likely to die as a result of full-term pregnancy than from a termination. Legal abortion is one of the safest operations available, with a death rate between one in every 100,000-200,000 procedures, and a morbidity rate of between 3-10 per cent.

There are too many abortions
The abortion rate in Britain is lower than in many other countries. Around 13 women in every 1000 have an abortion every year. It is calculated that in countries without legal abortion, the rates are generally higher.

There are too many late abortions
In 1991, 2.5 per cent of abortions were done after 20 weeks. These terminations can only be done for very serious reasons.

The law makes abortion too easy
Making abortion harder to get does

not reduce the numbers. In 1990, the law was changed and made very slightly more liberal. In 1991, numbers fell by 4 per cent compared with 1990.

There are no problems and no need to campaign to keep abortion legal
Anti-abortionists are constantly attempting to change the law – some 16 times since the 1967 Act was passed. Without campaigning by the National Abortion Campaign and our sister organisations, we might not have even the inadequate law we do have.

But it is not just from Parliament that the dangers come. Anti-abortion groups have tremendous resources which they use to try and persuade women that abortion is dangerous and traumatic – despite all the mass of research evidence to the contrary – thus helping to create needless stress and worry to women seeking to end unwanted pregnancies. Some extremists go further, harassing women and clinic staff outside clinics or even invading clinics. The fact is that we need constant vigilance if abortion rights are to be maintained and improved.

Pro-choice campaigners are in it for the money
Over half of all abortions are done on the NHS and most of the rest are done in clinics run by non-profit making charities. Compared to most private medicine, non-NHS abortions are not expensive. None of the organisations actively campaigning for improvements in the law and in provision are funded other than by their members and supporters, most of whom are women, who on average earn less than men and certainly are not rich. The National Abortion Campaign, like the other groups, is run on a shoestring.

That is why if you are pro-choice, your active support is so necessary. By joining NAC, you help to ensure that it is able to carry on campaigning to defend and improve abortion law and defend the improved women's access to abortion facilities.

Key issue – abortion

Information from the Society for the Protection of Unborn Children (SPUC)

The unborn child and the right to live

Abortion kills children. Abortion is the deliberate killing of an unborn child. Abortion denies the most basic of human rights, the right to life, that is due in justice to all members of the human family.

(The term 'abortion' is typically used to mean deliberate, or induced abortion, as opposed to 'spontaneous abortion', which is a natural miscarriage.)

The humanity of the unborn child

Birth does not mark the beginning of a new life, but the emergence of that individual from the womb. A new life begins in the womb (usually in the womb's fallopian tube) when an ovum (egg) from the mother is fertilised by a single sperm cell from the father. At fertilisation (conception), a new, unique, living human individual is present.

The developing baby (called a zygote at the single-cell stage, an embryo up to the end of the eighth week, and a foetus from nine weeks until birth) is not part of the mother any more than he or she is part of the father. At conception all the hereditary characteristics of the new human being are established: eye colour, sex, build, etc.

Nothing further is needed to direct the development of the embryo: all the information about how the baby is to grow and develop is contained in the original single cell at conception. Nothing is added after conception except oxygen and nutrients (food and water), the same essentials that are needed to sustain our life at all stages. From the beginning of the ninth week the term foetus is used to indicate that the developing child, whose body is now essentially complete, is recognisable to the eye as a human baby in miniature.

Birth is thus a change in the baby's environment, not a change in

SOCIETY FOR THE PROTECTION OF UNBORN CHILDREN

the nature of the baby. Humanity is not acquired but is inherent in all members of the human race.

The injustice of abortion

SPUC opposes abortion as an injustice to the unborn child and a denial of all his or her human rights. The right to life is an inalienable right – a right of which an innocent human being may not be deprived. Disability, social problems or the painful circumstances of a child's conception demand a compassionate response involving commitment to the welfare of both mother and child. True compassion is incompatible with taking innocent human life.

Not only is abortion a grave injustice in itself, it also perpetuates other social injustices. Abortion itself does not solve the social problems which lead women to seek abortions (such as unstable relationships, poor housing and financial insecurity). Rather, it undermines the will of society – at the levels of family, peer group and government – to find humane solutions which do not involve killing a baby.

The life of the mother

All human life is of equal value. The life of the child in the womb is neither more nor less important than the life of the mother, but equally so. There is therefore no moral objection to measures aimed solely at curing a life-threatening condition in an expectant mother, even if this may indirectly lead to the child's death. The ethical treatments available in such circumstances (for example, ectopic pregnancy in the fallopian tube) do not involve deliberately killing the baby. Serious medical problems which may arise later in pregnancy (when the child is capable of surviving outside the womb) may justify early delivery of the child, provided that appropriate steps are taken to save the life of the baby.

Abortion's victims

Abortion is typically carried out by the dismemberment, poisoning and/or the premature expulsion of the unborn child. It is usually an invasive procedure for the mother, which even in the best hospital conditions carries risks to her physical health, and often causes her psychological harm. Fathers and other family members may also suffer after an abortion, the ethics of healthcare professionals who take part in abortions are compromised, and society as a whole is harmed by the toleration of violence against the unborn child.

Early abortifacients

Abortion can also be caused in the first two weeks of life by methods of birth control which prevent the successful implantation of an embryo in the mother's womb. Although advocates of such techniques typically refer to this action as 'contraceptive', it nevertheless causes the death of an embryo in the womb and is therefore, by definition, abortifacient. Although the principle of contraception is outside SPUC's remit, the Society opposes abortifacient methods. The 'morning after pill' is primarily intended to work in this way, but other forms of the pill, intra-uterine device (coil), birth control implants and birth control vaccines can also cause abortion.

Ethical principles

Abortion is contrary to the medical ethics laid down in the Hippocratic Oath, both in its original version, derived from ancient Greece, and modern reformulations such as the World Medical Association's 1948 Declaration of Geneva. The Declaration states: 'I will maintain the utmost respect for human life, from the time of conception.' The right to life of all members of the human family is acknowledged in internationally agreed conventions and covenants, such as the Universal Declaration of Human Rights (1949) and the International Covenant on Civil and Political Rights (1976), as well as the 1959 Declaration of the Rights of the Child which explicitly applies this to the child before birth.

SPUC opposes abortion as an injustice to the unborn child and a denial of all his or her human rights

Our opposition to abortion, therefore, is based on ethical principles that have received universal approbation, and does not depend on the teachings of particular religions or denominations. All major world religions promote the value of life, and our membership reflects this, but the Society is not allied to any particular faith.

Questions you ask about abortion

Information from the National Abortion Campaign (NAC)

The National Abortion Campaign (NAC) came into existence in 1975 and very soon afterwards we started to get school students and others writing to us asking for our views on various aspects of abortion. The following information is based on over 20 years of answering queries about our views.

Introduction

Every time a woman is pregnant and is not sure whether or not she wants to have a baby, she has to make up her mind what she is going to do. Whatever her decision, the chances are that it can never be 100% satisfactory – like most things in real life. What women and those trying to help them attempt to do is to ensure the best outcome in each particular case.

Understanding the issues involved can help you prepare for making similar decisions, or in helping friends trying to make such difficult decisions, or simply in shaping your attitudes towards women who have faced this dilemma.

Is abortion murder?

Abortion can only be thought of as 'murder' if you believe that the foetus is a person. And even if you believe that it may be a person, with the same rights as the woman, abortion can be viewed as self-defence on the part of the woman who decides to have an abortion – she does so because she believes that the pregnancy threatens her in some way.

Even before abortion was made legal under certain circumstances, it was not legally murder and was treated differently under the law.

People have different views about the 'personhood' of the foetus. Politicians, religious leaders, doctors, scientists and philosophers have never been able to agree. There is no 'right' answer. Sometimes, anti-abortionists argue that therefore we should give the 'benefit of the doubt' to the foetus and assume that it is a person. The problem with this argument is, first, that this will not prevent women having 'backstreet abortions' – and these are likely to be dangerous and may be life-threatening – and, second, it assumes that we are prepared to impose our beliefs (or, in this case, doubts) on others, however strongly they disagree with us. So at the end of the day, it must be the individual's choice.

Of course the foetus is alive, and it could develop into a human being, but research shows that about 50-70% of all conceptions end in early miscarriage, often even before the woman is aware that she is pregnant. Clearly, the foetus is a potential human being, not an actual one.

Many women who have abortions have mixed feelings about what they are doing. It is seldom an easy decision and for some women it is a fact that under different circumstances they would not have the abortion. Sometimes women may regret having had an abortion, and sometimes women who decide not to have an abortion regret that decision too.

Doesn't the foetus/baby have any rights?

Of course it does. It has the right to be born wanted. There is ample evidence that throughout history women have tried to control the number of children they have and when they have them, through using contraception and abortion, often at great risk to their own lives and health. They know that if they are to be able to look after their children properly, they must control the number they have, both from the point of view of their own health and the resources they have – their income, housing, etc. Often it is only because of pressure from men in their society and family – who may want them to have more children, especially boys – that women have as many children as they do. A survey by the World Health Organisation showed that in many parts of the world women want smaller families than is the custom for their society.

Some research has been done into what happens to children who are born unwanted. In this country, like many where abortion is legal, a great many statistics are kept about women who have abortions, but none at all about those whose requests are refused, so we don't know how many of them there are and how many go on to have babies, or what happens to those babies. In Sweden before the second world war abortion was legal, but women had to go before hospital boards and plead their case, so there were records of women who were turned down. Some of them went on to have illegal abortions, but a study was made of a group of women who continued with their pregnancies after being refused abortion, and they, their families, and the children born as a result were compared to a similar group of women who had not sought abortion. It was found that the children born after their mothers had been refused an abortion generally did worse on every count – education, jobs, even their marriages did not last as long! And this disadvantage extended to their families, because their parents' marriage was also more likely to break up. Boys in particular were more likely to die in their teens or early twenties. A later study done in Yugoslavia found similar results.

Recent research into children who are adopted or taken into care shows that many of them have particular problems as well; children in care in this country are likely to have many foster families or end up going from one institution to another. Many of the homeless young people causing concern at the moment have been in care or have been fostered.

In considering whether or not to have an abortion, most women take the quality of life of their future child into consideration. For each woman in each society, this will be different, but throughout the world women want the best for their children. For most women, they think of this as a basic right for any children they may have, and this is why they try so hard to plan their families.

But isn't it better to have been born than not to be?

This is really a nonsense question. If you haven't been born, you don't know you might have been born, do you?

In any case, even many of those who have been born wish they had not, and take their own lives – including many very young people.

This question is asked by anti-abortionists to make us feel insecure, but in fact your existence – as YOU – is not dependent simply on the fact that your mother decided not to abort you, but on all sorts of factors which determined which particular egg from your mother met a particular sperm from your father – and of course, their existence depended on similar factors, right back to the start of the human race. Throughout that time, women have used abortion to control the size of their families, but you still got born, as did many billions of others, good, bad, famous, unknown, those who lived to be a hundred and those who barely drew breath before dying.

Why should it be just the woman's right to decide – what about husbands, boyfriends and doctors?

Women usually make up their mind about abortion after talking it over with people they trust and whose opinion they respect. That may well include their partner, or a parent, or a doctor. Often they prefer to talk to a complete stranger – someone who is not emotionally involved with their decision. But it is the woman who is pregnant, who at the end of the day must make the decision whether to have the baby and then decide whether to keep it or give it up for adoption, or to have an abortion. No one else should be allowed to force a woman either into having a baby she doesn't want or having an abortion she doesn't want.

There have been – and there still are – societies which, by making abortion illegal and contraception illegal or difficult to get, in practice force women to have babies they do not want and may not be able to care for properly. These have included some of the most totalitarian societies ever known, such as Hitler's Germany and South Africa under apartheid. Hitler, for example, wanted to increase the number of 'pure' Germans so German women were given awards for having lots of babies, and severely punished if they were discovered to have had an abortion. However, 'non-Germans' could be subjected to hideous experiments, which included abortions and sterilisation. Both groups were not allowed to make their own choices – one group was forced to have babies they did not want and the other had their right to have babies taken away from them.

There have been a number of legal cases in this country when men have tried to challenge their partner's right to have an abortion. In every case, the man has lost, because the courts realise that the best person to make the decision is the woman who actually has to bear the baby.

Deadly questions

Information from the Christian Medical Fellowship (CMF)

By Peter Saunders, CMF Student Secretary

1. Isn't the foetus only a potential human being?

This is the key issue. Biologically the foetus is undoubtedly human; it has human chromosomes derived from human gametes. It is also alive, exhibiting movement, respiration, sensitivity, growth, reproduction, excretion and nutrition. It is therefore more accurate to speak of it as a human being with potential, a human being in an early stage of development or a potential adult rather than a potential human being. Any biology text book tells us that human development is a continuous process beginning with fertilisation; essentially the only differences between zygote and full-term baby are nutrition and time.

The Bible makes many specific references to life before birth. Psalm 139[1] affirms God's creation of and communion with the unborn child. It also implies the continuity between life before and after birth: 'For you created my inmost being; you knit me together in my mother's womb . . . My frame was not hidden from you when I was made . . . your eyes saw my unformed body.'

God called Isaiah and Jeremiah before birth[2] and formed Job 'in the womb' as well as bringing him out of it.[3] Furthermore we have the Holy Spirit's own testimony[4] that Christ was present in Mary's womb at about 14 days' gestation.[5] Many other verses in the Bible reinforce these principles[6] and there are over 60 references that mention conception specifically.

Biologically and biblically, the foetus is a human being.

2. How can a non-sentient being have value?

Peter Singer, editor of the *Bioethics Journal*, puts the secular view of humanity in a nutshell: 'Once the religious mumbo-jumbo surrounding the term "human" has been stripped away . . . we will not regard as sacrosanct the life of every member of our species, no matter how limited its capacity for intelligent or even conscious life may be.'[7] To Singer and many influential thinkers like him, man is nothing but the product of matter, chance and time in a godless universe; merely a highly specialised animal. The value of an individual human being is determined by his level of rationality, self-consciousness, physical attributes or capacity for relationships. Human life that has fewer of these qualities is of less value and can be disposed of. This Darwinian ethic with its aim of 'survival of the fittest' puts the demented, mentally handicapped, brain-injured and unborn in great danger.

By contrast, the Christian view is that all human beings are made in God's image.[8] If they lack the means to feel, think or form relationships as we do, they still have dignity by virtue of the fact that they are made and known by God. Biblical morality dictates that the weak deserve special protection.[9] In God's economy the strong lay down their lives for the weak.[10] After all, protecting the vulnerable is what 'knowing God' is all about.[11] Even if it could be established that foetuses feel nothing, should it really make a difference to the way we treat them? Does anaesthesia legitimise killing?

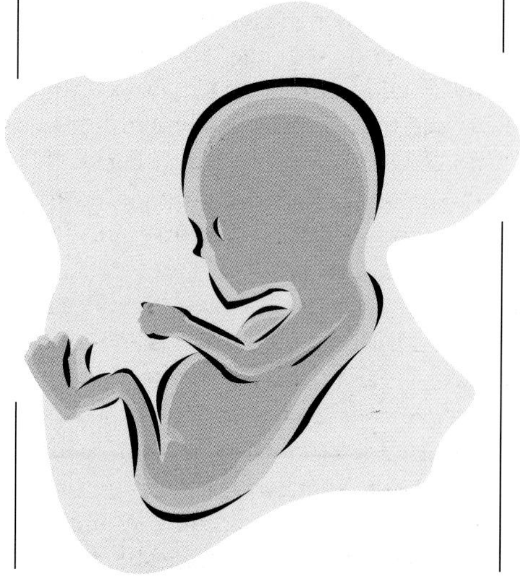

Having said this, we do not even know that the foetus is 'non-sentient'. We do know that brain function, as measured by EEG, is present in the foetus about six weeks after conception[12] and that responses to tactile sensation (skin tightening, bending, fist forming) can be observed at seven to eight weeks' gestation. At nine to ten weeks the foetus squints and swallows; breathing movements begin at eleven to twelve weeks. By 16 weeks he will respond violently to stimuli that you or I would find painful. Pain is a peculiarly personal and subjective experience: there is no biochemical or physiological test we can do to tell us if foetuses (or other people) experience it. By the same token we lack any proof that animals feel pain but judging by their responses, it seems charitable to assume that they do. No one would dare suggest dismembering newborn kittens (which ironically are born blind, deaf and helpless at nine weeks' gestation!).

3. Don't women have a right to choose?

Any woman with an unplanned pregnancy will understandably feel under pressure, especially if the father of the child is not supportive. Whether she opts for abortion, adoption or keeping the baby, her decision will change her life for ever. She needs to know that the foetus is not just 'part of her body'. It is a genetically distinct and vulnerable human being that has come into existence, almost always, because of choices she and her partner have made.

Some argue that only women can decide about abortion because only women understand what it is like to be pregnant. While this has a certain validity it also has shortcomings. It is rather like arguing that only drivers should be able to decide about road rules because only drivers understand the pressures of driving. However, the actions of motorists can have profound effects on passengers, bystanders and the drivers of other cars as well. In the same way there is a 'passenger' in the womb and other parties outside it to consider.

No man (or woman) is an island. We all value the opportunity of living in a free society but also recognise that personal autonomy has its limits. Rights need protection but they are not absolute. They must be balanced against responsibilities. We are not free to do things which limit or violate the reasonable freedoms of others. In human community abortion is not simply a matter between a woman and her doctor. There are others to consider: the father, any other citizens who may be affected by the decision and, not least, the unborn child herself.

Although there are exceptions, most unwanted pregnancies result from a conscious decision to engage in sexual intercourse by people who are equipped neither for pregnancy nor parenthood (67% of women having abortions in Britain have never been married).[13] It is only natural to regret wrong decisions made in the heat of the moment; however, killing an innocent human being to avert the consequences of choices we have made is never morally justifiable. The right to life is the most fundamental right of all.

Solo mothers will need support, and adoption even with its difficulties is always an option to consider. There are many childless couples spending thousands of pounds on infertility treatments because babies they could have provided a home for have been among the 4.8 million terminated in Britain since 1968.

4. Won't refusing abortion simply mean that women suffer?

A common myth is that women will not change their minds about having an abortion when offered practical help and given the facts about foetal development. Many do, and pregnancy counselling organisations like CARE for Life[14] have made a substantial contribution in helping women whose turning to abortion is simply a cry for help. Even women refused abortions do not necessarily seek them. An early Swedish study[15] of 4274 women refused abortion showed that 85.6% completed their pregnancies and only 10% sought an abortion elsewhere.[16] Another similar study followed up 249 such women for 7 to 10 years finding that 73% were satisfied with the way things had turned out; 69% were taking care of the child.[17] Most unwanted pregnancies, if not aborted, result in wanted children. Conversely most abused children come from wanted pregnancies. Since the Abortion Act came into force in Britain in 1968 the incidence of child abuse has doubled.[18]

Many believe that women refused abortion are at risk of mental illness. However, representatives of the Royal College of Psychiatry giving evidence to the Rawlinson Commission[19] have stated that there are no psychiatric grounds for abortion. This is in spite of the fact that most abortions are carried out on alleged grounds of damage to the mother's mental health. In fact, for suicidal pregnant women, abortion will increase depression and the risk of post-abortion psychosis.[20] What they really need is proper psychiatric treatment. As a general rule pregnancy enhances rather than damages mental health; the incidence of suicide in non-pregnant women of childbearing age is 18 times that in pregnant women.[21]

While first trimester abortions are usually physically safe (for the mother), complications do however occur: uterine perforation, haemorrhage, sepsis, cervical lacerations and retained placentae in the short term as well as chronic pelvic inflammatory disease, subfertility, cervical incompetence, rhesus isoimmunisation and menstrual disturbances in the long term. A prospective and joint RCGP/RCOG study showed that 10% of women had complications within three weeks of the procedure.[22] As complications are required to be reported by one week, and most occur after this time, the rate may well be higher. Women damaged by abortion are unlikely to return to the institution that damaged them simply to be counted.

Early psychiatric morbidity appears to be about 10%.[23] The long-term sequelae are difficult to evaluate as follow-up rates are low for a variety of reasons, not least that many do not wish to be reminded of their experience. In some patients post-abortion psychosis can be crippling and those who feel ambiguous about the decision are particularly vulnerable.[24]

References

1. Ps 139:13-16
2. Is 49:1; Je 1:5
3. Jb 10:8-9, 18-19
4. Lk 1:42
5. Lk 1:36, 56-58
6. Gn 25:22-23; Ps 22:9-10, 51:5, 71:6; Ec 11:5; Ho 12:3
7. Singer P. Sanctity of Life or Quality of Life? *Paediatrics* 1983;72(1):128-9
8. Gn 1:27, 9:6
9. Pr 22:22-23; Ex 21:2-6, 22:21-24; Lv 19:14,32
10. Phil 2:5-8; Rom 5:6-8
11. Je 22:16,17
12. *NEJM* 1982; p564 (26 August)
13. Whelan R. *Legal Abortion Examined.* SPUC Ed Res Trust 1992
14. Minnis S. GPs and Crisis Pregnancy Counselling Centres. *Nucleus* 1996; January:15-21
15. Hultgren G. Refusal of Request for Legal Abortion. *Nord Med* 1957;62: 1182-85
16. Sweden legalised abortion in the 1930s.
17. Hook K. Refused abortion. *Acta Psychiat Scand* 1963;suppl 168:3-156
18. Whelan R. op cit
19. Rawlinson Report. *The Physical & Psychosocial Effects of Abortion on Women.* London,1994
20. *Psychiatric Journal of the University of Ottawa* 1989;14:506-16
21. *BMJ* 1991;302:126-7
22. Frank P et al. *J R Coll Gen Pract* 1985;92:308-16
23. Zolese G, Blacker CVR. The psychological complications of therapeutic abortion. *Brit J Psych*;1992;160:742-749
24. Rawlinson Report. Op cit

• The above is an extract from the magazine *Nucleus*, the Student Journal of the Christian Medical Fellowship (CMF).

Anti-choice questions: Pro-choice answers

We don't need an active pro-choice campaign in Britain, do we?
The overwhelming majority of the British people are in favour of legal abortion, yet most of the recent publicity around abortion has been generated by anti-choice groups, which has created the impression that these groups have more support than they actually do. Women's right to abortion has been under sustained attack; it is important for people who agree that women should have safe, free, equal access to abortion on request to campaign actively for it.

Aren't pro-choice people pro-abortion?
No: we think that women faced with an unwanted pregnancy should have the right to choose whether or not to continue the pregnancy. We also believe that sex education, and information and research into safe, effective contraception, should be promoted. Pro-choice people have no interest in increasing the number of abortions taking place in Britain; we believe that women should have the right to make the choice.

Don't women living in the UK already have the right to choose abortion?
No: women are not considered legally competent to make that decision for themselves; they need two doctors to decide that their particular abortion is legal under the terms of the 1967 Abortion Act. Wanting, or requesting, an abortion is not sufficient grounds for an abortion in the UK under the law as it stands at present.

Now that contraception is widely available, don't women who get pregnant have only themselves to blame?
Anyone expressing this view is ignoring the fact that all contraceptives – even properly used, effective ones – occasionally fail. Also, contraceptives are still not as

widely available as they should be, especially for young people, and neither is good sex education. In many cases women cannot always insist that contraceptives are used. But more importantly, this view seems to support the idea that women should be punished for their pregnancy by being forced to carry that pregnancy to term – motherhood should not be seen as some kind of social disciplinary measure.

Abortion is the killing of an unborn child: how can that be justified?
This statement is true for people who believe that personhood begins at the moment of conception. A fertilised egg, or a foetus, has the potential to become a person, but that is not the same thing as being a person. Those who express this view put the foetus at the centre of the problem faced by women who have an unwanted pregnancy; over 80% of the UK population believe that the woman is at the centre of this problem, and should, therefore, be able to make the decision. As the pregnancy progresses, and the foetus develops, abortion becomes medically more difficult; those people who are really concerned about this should join NAC in our campaign to make abortion more widely available early on in the pregnancy; so that late abortions – already relatively rare – become less frequent.

Abortion is dangerous to women's health, isn't it?
No: an early abortion is many times safer than childbirth, and women who have had a legal abortion are just as likely to have a healthy baby in the future as other women. There are countries where abortion is very dangerous indeed – world-wide it has been estimated that 200,000 women die every year as a direct result of unsafe abortion. Unsafe abortion happens in countries where abortion is illegal, and there should be no doubt that anti-choice campaigners would like to see the UK become one of these countries.

Do you deny that abortion is harmful to women psychologically?
Absolutely: the vast majority of women experience relief following an abortion which they have requested. The risk to a woman's

mental health are far greater if she is refused a wanted abortion than if she can access one. A minority of women do experience regret after an abortion, but this is often related to the circumstances in her life which meant that she was unable to have a child at that particular time. Research has demonstrated that, when counselling is available for women who are undecided about what to do with an unplanned pregnancy, and women are enabled to make an informed decision, psychological problems are extremely rare.

Isn't adoption the perfect solution for women with unwanted pregnancies?

No. Of course it is an option, but in a democratic society this should be a matter of choice. Women should never be forced to bear children for other people to adopt.

Don't pro-choice people support abortion in any circumstances?

What pro-choice people support is the right of women to make this decision for themselves, believing that women are in the best position to decide whether or not they can carry this pregnancy to term, and care for a child for the next 18 years. There may be individual circumstances in which some women may make this complex decision differently than might others; in a democratic society such differences should be recognised and defended. The alternative is to set up a system whereby individual women are judged on how good their reason for requesting an abortion appears to be. This will always create injustice, as some women will be better able to come up with good reasons than will others, when, in fact, most women's reasons tend to result from their inability to carry to term a particular pregnancy at a particular time. Women should not be forced to demonstrate varying degrees of anguish in order to 'qualify' for an abortion, which is what such a system would demand of women.

Does NAC support time limits of any kind on abortion?

NAC believes that the key to reducing the incidence of late abortion is to make early abortion easier for women to obtain. This is borne out by the experience of women in European countries where abortion on request is available. NAC does not believe that it is necessary for governments to impose time limits. 89% of abortions in the UK are carried out in the first 13 weeks of pregnancy. Women want their abortions to be performed as early as possible. In some cases, there may be compelling medical or other reasons as to why an abortion may be needed at any time during the pregnancy; to legislate in such a way that late abortions would be illegal would criminalise doctors and possibly women, and would not be sound medical practice.

Abortion is morally wrong, isn't it?

Many people believe that it is morally wrong to bring an unwanted child into the world. The vast majority of people in Britain believe abortion to be a humane and responsible decision.

Did NAC welcome the publicity that the launch of an anti-abortion political party brought to the issue of abortion?

No. The anti-abortion party descended to new depths of duplicity in their campaign, which manipulated lurid pictures in an attempt to induce guilt among women and men who believe that abortion is a valid option. As a result, pro-choice activists had to respond to the claims of these anti-abortionists who gained publicity which was out of all proportion to the support they have in the country, given that their first goal is to repeal the 1967 Abortion Act. Only a tiny minority of the population share this view (4% strongly disagree with a woman's right to choose an abortion, MORI August 1996, as opposed to 81% who agree or strongly agree).

NAC would like to see equal access to abortion for women throughout the country

Is NAC in favour of pregnancy counselling?

Yes, we believe all women should have access to non-directive counselling if they want it, but not the type of 'counselling' endorsed by anti-abortionists, which tends to take the form of 'counsellors' showing pregnant women distorted pictures of foetuses, usually at a later stage of gestation than they claim, and anti-abortion films. They also claim women will suffer from 'post abortion trauma'. Their 'pavement counselling' techniques involve harassing women trying to enter abortion clinics. NAC believes that some women know that they want to have an abortion, and do not need counselling in order to make up their minds. For those who are undecided, non-directive pregnancy counselling, which explores all of the options, including maintaining the pregnancy, and allows the woman to make her own decision, can be very valuable.

So what changes would NAC like to see to the 1967 Abortion Act?

NAC believes that the 1967 Act was right for the 1960s, but wrong for the 1990s. We believe that abortion should be available on request in the belief that only then will women have the legal right to make this decision for themselves. At the moment, the availability of abortion in Britain is, to a large degree, dependent on the attitude of the health authority in the area where you live. NAC would like to see equal access to abortion for women throughout the country.

Isn't NAC the mirror image of anti-abortion groups?

No; the essential difference between us is that we believe in the right of women to choose, or not to choose, abortion, as they see fit. Anti-abortion groups believe in their fight to impose their extreme and very unpopular views on all women. They aim to change the law to force women into either continuing with an unwanted pregnancy or endangering their lives and health by seeking an illegal abortion.

Young girls need facts

Unless abortion is positively promoted, 12-year-olds will continue to have babies

By Polly Toynbee

The tale of the 12-year-old girl from Rotherham who has just given birth, making her mother a grandmother at 26, sends out shock waves. The story gets worse, as yesterday police were questioning the mother's ex-lover over paternity of the girl's baby. And even worse when it emerges that the mother herself gave birth to her fifth child a few weeks ago, an appalling vision of a calamitous family.

Whatever social policies we devise, human society will always produce bizarre and terrible cases: whatever can happen, will happen somewhere. We don't know if anything could have saved this 12-year-old from her fate. But maybe really good sex education from a very young age might have made a difference. Maybe confidential and friendly counselling from a school nurse would have been a lifeline. And if she had been taught about abortion in a positive and open way, she might have escaped this disaster.

Rotherham, with one of the highest teenage pregnancy rates, will be a good test of the government's promise to halve teenage pregnancies in the next 10 years. Nationally each year 63 in every 1000 girls under the age of 20 get pregnant, more than 94,000 girls. The most worrying statistic is what teenagers do when they get pregnant. Overall, only 37% opt for abortion. Worse still, only half of all girls who get pregnant under 16 have abortions. Middle-class girls are twice as likely to choose termination – double the number in Surrey than in Barnsley, for example. But there is a real problem persuading girls that abortion is the best solution.

It's not hard to see why. Thirty years after legalisation, it is still shrouded in moral ambiguity, with teachers and the medical profession often afraid to promote it strongly to young girls. Abortion may be the last resort, but girls need telling that it is better than a blighted life as a schoolgirl mother with a dismal outlook for her children. It is not enough to inform them neutrally about abortion. It needs to be promoted positively without fear of intimidation from the small but extraordinarily powerful and frightening anti-abortion lobby.

Education for Choice is a struggling organisation offering pro-abortion information to schools. Its excellent new information pack and video have just been published, trying to counteract the welter of propaganda from anti-abortion groups which bombards schoolchildren. Girls are easily influenced by these 'pro-life' emotional and mendacious videos, with frightening warnings that abortion causes infertility. But to put the pro-abortion case Education for Choice has no money.

Disgracefully, it has been refused any funds from both the health and education departments, which took fright at the very idea. The teaching pack costs £15 and the video £25, while the very well funded anti-abortionists offer all theirs for free. In most schools, abortion remains an almost taboo subject beyond debates in RE classes, denying honest, unemotional, practical information.

At their most sentimental and veggie stage, girls are easily influenced by images of murdered babies. It takes a great deal of discussion and hard fact to persuade them that a foetus in the early weeks is not a baby, and that nature itself aborts large numbers without women even knowing they were pregnant.

Of course some girls will have deep religious objections. But most will change their minds as they get older: opinion surveys show young girls are far more anti-abortion than older, wiser women, who are strongly in favour. Unwanted pregnancy is a fact of women's lives, not a rare mistake. One in four women will have an abortion at some time and yet it still usually remains a shameful secret.

The new ministerial task force on teenage pregnancy has yet to meet. When it does will it dare to look honestly at the whole question? Britain was a pioneer in legalisation, but now lags behind. (Abortion on request is the norm in Europe.) What once seemed progressive is now archaic, drenched in disapproval,

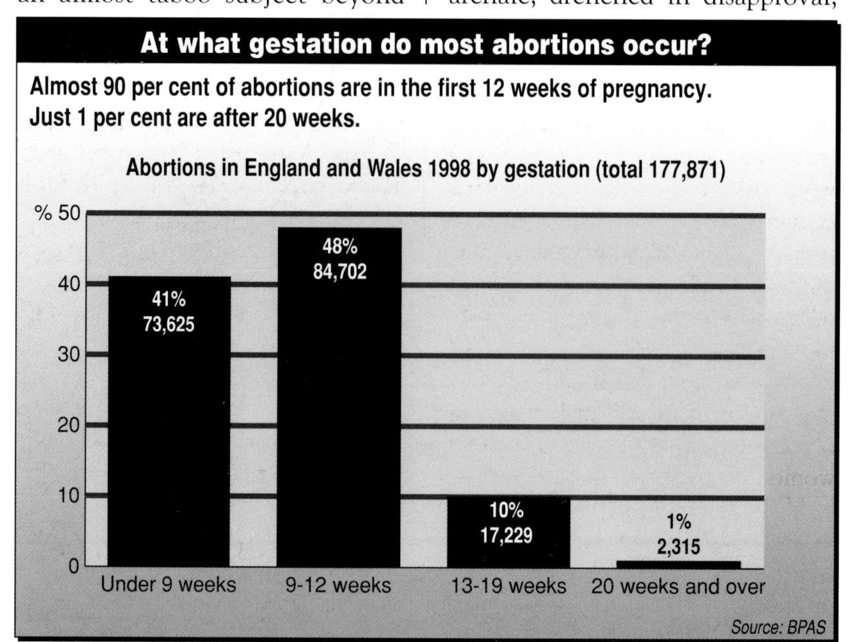

creating deliberate obstacles, setting a tone of shame that makes it an equivocal subject for schools.

The law demands a woman must pretend to two doctors that she is on the point of a nervous breakdown in order to get their signatures. It suggests she is committing a sin, unless absolved on medical grounds. But why should doctors decide whether a woman should become a mother against her will? Doctors, like everyone else, have their own views; as a result, 27% of women are forced into paying for private abortions, usually because disapproving doctors prevaricate.

Women are treated by the law as irresponsible children or lunatics. Odd that they are presumed responsible enough to be unwilling mothers, but not to make the choice. I used to think it better to let this sleeping dog lie, since although the law is bad, at least most women who seek abortions do eventually get one, even if they have to pay. Do we really want to rouse up the old enemy for yet another bible-bashing, plastic-foetus-waving, furious debate with the religious minority?

But I now think we will never get an open and honest approach to unwanted pregnancy, to easy contraception and the morning-after pill until we finally lay all this nonsense to rest.

Only a woman herself can decide what to do when confronted with the disaster of accidental pregnancy. Changing the law to reflect that would change the moral climate. As long as women have the shaming obligation of pretending to doctors that they are half-mad, the climate of sin, disapproval and fear will remain.

The same mumbo-jumbo prevents the morning-after pill and oral contraceptives being available over the counter at chemist's. The medical profession is used as a moral gatekeeper on sexual matters that are none of its business, and should refuse to do it. Medical mystique frightens off the most vulnerable and the youngest.

The Pro-Choice Alliance, an umbrella campaign, is looking for an MP brave enough to take up abortion reform as a private member's bill. Many have expressed strong support, but Labour MPs are under heavy pressure from above not to touch it. Meanwhile we wait to see how vigorous and brave the new task force will be over the whole fraught question of sex education and making contraception easy to get.

Tessa Jowell and the health department are keen, but the auguries from David Blunkett are not good, with a press release this week saying he regards sex education as a matter primarily for parents. However, 96% of parents regard it as the school's duty, and of all educational failures, 94,000 teenage pregnancies must be the worst.

- Education for Choice can be contacted at 18 Ashwin St, London, E8 3DL, or e-mail them at efc@efc.org.uk

Most GPs 'now back abortion on demand'

By Aisling Irwin, Medical Correspondent

The number of GPs who support 'abortion on demand' has increased over the past 25 years, says a study published today.

Sixty per cent of family doctors now believe a woman should be able automatically to have an abortion in the first three months of pregnancy if she wants it. In 1973, the figure was 24 per cent. Pro-choice campaigners will use the figures to support a call today for the law to be changed in favour of abortion on demand for women in their first three months of pregnancy.

They also want GPs to be obliged to declare any conscientious objections to abortion and to refer women to a doctor who does not hold the same view.

The study was commissioned by Marie Stopes International, which provides family planning services including abortion, and is part of a campaign to liberalise the 1967 Abortion Act. Overseen by Prof Colin Francome, a health sociologist, the study obtained the opinions of 1,000 GPs around Britain and another 2,300 in selected regions.

More than eight out of 10 GPs described themselves as 'broadly pro-choice', with most of the rest – one in five – 'broadly anti-abortion'. Of the latter group, a fifth said they supported a woman's 'right to choose'. Three-quarters of GPs thought women should be entitled to free NHS abortions.

Marie Stopes International said it had unearthed a 'massive sea change' in GPs' views since the study in 1973. Helen Axby, Marie Stopes International's chief executive, said five per cent of GPs were both anti-abortion and reluctant to declare their position to a woman patient.

'We are disturbed by the finding that a significant minority of GPs may be imposing their own moral standards and values on women, causing distress, delay and financial hardship.' Life, the leading anti-abortion charity, said the report was 'extremely suspect'.

- Women on the Pill are not being warned by doctors that they risk becoming pregnant if they take antibiotics. Studies show that 136 pregnancies since 1967 were caused by taking the two substances together, say researchers in the *Journal of Accident and Emergency Medicine*.

Abortion guidelines hailed by campaigners

Royal college calls for operation within three weeks of referral

By Sarah Boseley, Health Correspondent

New guidelines on abortion were last night hailed by campaigners as a turning point in a service that has had to fight for legitimacy and is still often subject to stigma.

Ann Furedi of the British Pregnancy Advisory Service said the Royal College of Obstetricians and Gynaecologists' document setting new standards for the NHS and private clinics was a clear sign that the medical profession, policy makers and society at large were beginning to accept abortion as part of essential reproductive health care.

She added: 'Abortion may have been legal in Britain for 30 years but it has yet to be recognised as entirely legitimate and is often the subject of controversial debate. If the RCOG succeeds in establishing these principles of care nationally it will represent the "coming of age" of abortion services.'

The anti-abortion lobby is incensed by the suggestion that abortion could become respectable, and will shortly be even further angered by a booklet for children which the Family Planning Association plans to publish and distribute in schools. The booklet is in cartoon style and aimed at those in their early to middle teens. It describes what abortion is and the reasons why a girl might seek one.

Today's royal college guidelines, compiled by a group funded by the department of health, says abortion services should 'provide high quality, efficient, effective and comprehensive care that respects the dignity, individuality and rights of women to exercise personal choice over their treatment'.

Abortion is far more common than most people realise. Because of the stigma and shame attached, few women will talk about it, but the college points out that at least a third of women experience an abortion before the age of 45. Studies have shown that the majority are not young girls, but women in their twenties, and that a substantial number are older women who already have children. Organisations like the pregnancy advisory service – and the FPA with its booklet for children – think it is time for the normalisation of abortion which, they insist, nobody ever embarks upon lightly.

They are delighted that the college's guidelines emphasise the safety of the procedure. It is safer, the document states, than carrying a pregnancy to term, and complications are uncommon. But there is unequal access to abortion around the country and many women have to endure lengthy and distressing delays under the NHS. This, and the disapproval of some GPs, are the main reasons why many women resort to private clinics.

The guidelines state that no woman should have to wait longer than three weeks from her initial referral by the GP. Ideally, she should be offered an appointment for assessment within five days of referral and she should have the termination within seven days of her request being approved.

The document recommends that day-care services should be provided because they are cost-effective and can minimise disruption to the lives of women and their families. Some clinics have begun a lunch-hour service, which has been castigated by critics. The royal college suggests no more than 10% will need an overnight stay.

Wherever possible, women who are admitted for an abortion should be treated separately from those who are pregnant and want their baby – particularly if they are having an ultrasound scan. Putting them together can be distressing for both. Health authorities should provide more information to let women know how to obtain an abortion and what options are available to them.

The document, *The Care of Women requesting Induced Abortion*, suggests that psychological trauma is more common in women who have been denied an abortion than in those who have had one. 'Only a small minority of women experience any long-term adverse psychological sequelae after abortion,' it says. 'Early distress, although common, is usually a continuation of symptoms present before the abortion. Conversely, long-lasting, negative effects on both mothers and their children are reported where abortion has been denied.'

Family planning group shatters 'A' word taboo

By Jacqui Thornton

A family planning clinic has caused outrage by placing huge posters on the London Underground that bluntly use the word 'abortion'.

It is the first time that abortion services have been advertised so blatantly. A spokesman for the British Pregnancy Advisory Service said that abortion was a 'fact of life', a necessary back-up to contraception, and that the posters were nothing to be ashamed of.

The BPAS claims that it wants to break the taboo of what it calls 'the A word', and has spelled out ABORTION in posters 10ft by 7ft, using pictures of women's faces as letters. Below, it says that 55,000 women 'turned' to the BPAS last year.

Pro-life groups have reacted with fury, saying that abortion kills thousands of unborn children. Jack Scarisbrick, the director of Life, is complaining to the Advertising Standards Authority, while the ProLife Alliance is to ask London Underground to put up a similar-sized poster, of an aborted 21-week foetus.

The BPAS campaign by the advertising agency Prima Communications, which consists of 59 posters displayed on different sections of the Underground, is understood to have cost in the region of £25,000 for one month. The BPAS remains defiant. Ann Furedi, the director of communications, said it was insulting to claim that women who did not want abortions would be persuaded by the advertisements.

She said: 'The posters break a long tradition where the A word has been avoided for fear of offending those who disapprove of abortion. We believe it's time to break the taboo and challenge the notion that abortion is a problem. Abortion is simply a fact of life.

'Women should not have to feel ashamed or apologetic about needing abortion care, and we make no apologies for providing it. Abortion can be a legal, moral and responsible solution to an unwanted pregnancy. BPAS is proud to be Britain's largest single abortion provider.'

However, Mr Scarisbrick said that the poster showed the desperation of the BPAS, which he claimed was exploiting women's vulnerability. He said: 'Everyone knows that abortion is nasty. They may say they want to break the taboo of the A word but we know that women do not want abortions. They have abortions because of other people.'

'Women should not have to feel ashamed or apologetic about needing abortion care, and we make no apologies for providing it.'

Sarah Macken, the director of Student LifeNet, a pro-life group, said that the BPAS was engaging in a cynical marketing war against its rivals, Marie Stopes and others. She said: 'They seem to be saying abortion is normal. It is not a normal operation. It is simply for the intention of killing a lot of babies. It is not acceptable to advertise this in the same way that you would advertise make-up.'

Bruno Quintavalle, of the ProLife Alliance, said that his organisation's plan to ask London Underground to put up a poster of a foetus would test how much of a taboo there was about abortion. Mr Quintavalle said: 'We will be asking London Underground to put up our poster at the earliest opportunity. We have been planning a poster campaign for some time but this has brought forward our agenda.

'I find the BPAS poster extremely offensive. They are not putting forward one side of the picture, they are misrepresenting the horror of abortion. If they want a proper debate, we feel the reality has to be presented. We also want to get the issue out in the open.'

The Alliance believes that there is too much censorship of images of abortion and is waiting for a legal ruling from Europe on whether the picture of a foetus could be used in a political party broadcast. However Neil Byrne, a spokesman for London Underground, said the poster had passed the 'stringent' guidelines it lays down for advertising. He refused to reveal how much the BPAS had been charged.

He said: 'They are entitled to advertise their services as much as any business. Carrying as many people as we do, three million a day, it is hard not to offend somebody. When people submit posters we are aware that we carry large numbers of very young and older people with different views.

'We do turn people down but we did not think this was a distasteful poster. It is a service offering pregnancy advice. It is shock tactics but it is within the guidelines we find acceptable.'

The Advertising Standards Authority said that it would investigate any complaints thoroughly. It has the power to ban advertisements if complaints from members of the public or other bodies are upheld. Its code says that adverts must be decent, truthful, legal and honest and must not offend consumers.

Although it is illegal to advertise prescription medicines, there is no such law banning the promotion of family planning clinics which offer abortions. Chris Reid, a spokesman for the ASA, said: 'This is obviously a very sensitive and emotive issue.'

Women versus babies

By Ann Furedi

Throughout the 1970s, the arguments for a woman's right to choose seemed relatively straightforward. 'Free abortion on demand' was a central tenet of the women's liberation movement. It was understood that women needed to control their fertility if they were to participate in society on equal terms with men and, since contraception sometimes failed, legal abortion was essential if women were to enjoy their sexuality.

To argue against 'the right to choose' was to argue that women should fulfil their traditional domestic destiny as wives and mothers at a time when sexual freedom and women's economic independence were celebrated.

But today, abortion is no longer a left versus right, radical versus reactionary, feminist versus anti-feminist issue. Today, there are fewer 'fundamentalists' on either side. Just a tiny – if vocal – minority believe that abortion is always wrong. Even most of those who campaign for tighter legal restrictions concede that there are circumstances when abortion may be legitimate.

On the other side of the debate, there are fewer voices prepared to argue a robust defence of a woman's absolute right to choose abortion. Some believe abortion on grounds of abnormality is uncomfortably close to eugenics; sometimes a line is drawn at a particular gestational limit.

The issues surrounding late abortions are particularly contentious. Techniques in foetal medicine have made it easier to sustain the lives of severely premature babies. Infants can now be saved at gestations when foetuses can be legally aborted.

Increasingly, obstetricians talk of having two patients – the woman and the foetus. Discussions about the rights of the child (and, indeed, the rights of animals) have encouraged debates about what rights, if any, should be conferred on the foetus, while the abortion debates in the 1970s were about the social status of women.

In the past, law and religion defined our understanding because science had little to say, as science writer Greg Easterbrook argues in a recent US *New Republic* article. He claims the case for liberal provision of early abortion is strengthened by evidence that the natural termination of potential life is far more common than previously assumed – but scientific discoveries about the brain activity of the more developed foetus stand as an argument against late abortion.

Easterbrook believes this is a message the pro-choice movement does not want to hear lest they be compelled to trade off liberal earlier abortion for restrictions on those in later pregnancy.

Those of us who provide abortion services cannot afford to insulate ourselves from contemporary debates. For example, it is not uncommon for women seeking to end a pregnancy to be concerned about whether a procedure causes pain to the foetus. Our clinicians would be failing their profession if they were not aware of developments in neonatal medicine.

Because of the need for open debate, British Pregnancy Advisory Service hosted a meeting in London yesterday of almost 100 clinicians, academics, policy makers and campaigners, including those hostile to abortion, to consider the 'new ethics' of abortion.

Each year we provide nearly 55,000 abortions – most are in early pregnancy, but some are late. We see no need for apology or moral defensiveness. Rather we believe there is a strong case for trying to wrest the moral imperative away from those who assume they have the monopoly on ethical concerns.

Within the confines of the law we strive to allow women to exercise 'procreative autonomy', that is to assert their own control over if and when they have children. We believe that a civilised society accepts that women are creatures with a moral conscience, capable of making responsible decisions for themselves. This is as true for women who seek late abortions as it is for women in early pregnancy. Women do not request abortion because they are ignorant about foetal development but because, for some reason, they find their pregnancy intolerable.

Science may be making new discoveries about foetal development, but it has little to tell us about the real lives of women. The issue is not so much whether or when the embryo/foetus is deserving of respect *per se*, but how much respect and value we accord to a life (that does not even know it is alive) relative to the respect and value we have for the life of the woman who carries it.

Some argue that civilised society can be judged by its attitude to the 'unborn child'. We believe it can also be judged by its attitude to women.

• Ann Furedi is director of communications, British Pregnancy Advisory Service

Voice for Choice

The campaign to secure abortion on request throughout the UK

Introduction

Voice for Choice is a national campaign by the Pro-Choice Alliance, a coalition of organisations calling for long overdue reform of the 1967 Abortion Act. The campaign seeks to end the widespread discrimination and inequalities of access that occur in the National Health Service abortion provision, and to secure for all women in the United Kingdom the genuine right to decide for themselves whether or not to continue an unwanted pregnancy.

A change in the law will reflect views repeatedly voiced by the overwhelming majority of British people in favour of abortion on request; it will enable women to secure abortions earlier, when the procedures involved are particularly safe; it will bring the United Kingdom into line with the majority of its European partners; and it will help to increase the chance that in future every child born in the United Kingdom will be a wanted child and every woman with a crisis pregnancy will receive the non-judgmental, prompt, caring and supportive service to which she should be entitled.

A change in the law will increase the chance that every woman with a crisis pregnancy will receive the non-judgmental, prompt, caring and supportive service to which she should be entitled.

The current law

The 1967 Abortion Act allows abortion provided two doctors certify that the pregnancy has not exceeded its 24th week and that its continuance would place the woman, or any existing child of her family, at greater risk of physical or mental injury than if the pregnancy were terminated.

Abortion is legal after 24 weeks only where two doctors certify that there is a substantial risk of foetal abnormality or that abortion is necessary to save the woman from death or permanent injury.

Why we need reform: whose choice?

It is a popular misconception that the current law allows for abortion at the request of the woman concerned. In fact, an abortion is legal only if two doctors certify that it is necessary under the terms of the 1967 Act; unwanted pregnancy is not one of those terms.

Some doctors accept that an unwanted pregnancy is always potentially harmful and will support her requests for abortion for this reason. They are legally permitted to do this.

Other doctors may be judgemental, obstructive and unhelpful, delaying women or turning them away in circumstances where another doctor would consider an abortion to be warranted. They are legally permitted to do this.

By allowing doctors to exercise wide discretion and make personal judgements over women, the 1967 Abortion Act creates a climate of uncertainty and the potential for unfair and arbitrary discrimination. It places an additional, unjust emotional burden on women who may already be facing one of the most difficult and traumatic decisions of their lives.

Teenagers are particularly vulnerable, often delaying an approach to doctors in fear that their confidentiality may be compromised or that they will be lectured. Delay leaves them to experience the physical and emotional trauma of later abortion.

The law must be amended to recognise that the only person capable of deciding whether or not a pregnancy should continue is the person most directly affected by that decision – the woman herself.

Why we need reform: barriers to access

Recent studies in the United Kingdom have demonstrated the wide disparity in the provision of NHS abortion services in various parts of the country; the level of NHS provision ranges from more than 90% of local demand to less than 40% in some health authority areas. And, of course, in Northern Ireland, where the 1967 Abortion Act does not apply, both NHS and private sector provision is non-existent.

Some health authorities do not consider abortion services to be particularly important and accord them low priority for funding, which means they fail to meet the needs of local women. A woman with an unwanted pregnancy cannot *expect* to be referred for NHS abortion in the way that a woman with a wanted pregnancy *can expect* NHS ante-natal and maternity care.

Lack of access may have grave implications for women's health, since inadequate local NHS funding tends to result in long waiting lists, or arbitrary restrictions, such as refusing women who have previously had NHS abortions or who are beyond a certain number of weeks of pregnancy. Women in low income groups are particularly vulnerable, as they cannot resort to the private sector in the event that local NHS providers turn them away.

By placing a duty on health authorities to fully fund abortions for local women, the number of late abortions will be reduced, with a consequent reduction in physical complications and emotional traumas associated with later procedures.

Why we need reform: Northern Ireland

The women of Northern Ireland have to travel to Britain in order to secure abortion, because the 1967 Abortion Act does not extend to Northern Ireland. An average of 40 women every week make the journey to private clinics, largely travelling in secret, at great personal cost, both financially and emotionally. They are denied medical treatment legally available to other women in the United Kingdom, and will frequently be unable to obtain proper post-abortion care or counselling, because doctors in Northern Ireland – who are understandably dubious about their precarious legal position – are poorly trained in, and reluctant to deal with, the complications of abortion.

Implementing a right to access legal abortion services in Northern Ireland will end thirty years of the most blatant discrimination against a section of the United Kingdom community, and will reflect the public will of the people of Northern Ireland, who have consistently supported legal abortion.

Placing obstacles in women's ways doesn't help them or make them change their minds; it only makes the whole experience more distressing.

Why we need reform: union with Europe

In 1967, Britain led the world in framing a progressive legislation for abortion. The 1967 Abortion Act has since been superseded and rendered archaic and paternalistic by the legislative reforms made by Britain's European partners, most of which have introduced laws which provide for abortion on request in the first trimester of pregnancy.

There is no evidence that a liberal reform of abortion legislation will result in an increase in the numbers of women seeking to access the service. On the contrary, if coupled with progressive sex education programmes and access to comprehensive family planning services, the evidence suggests an opposite effect, as experience from the Netherlands and Finland, where abortion rates are among the lowest in the world, clearly demonstrates.

The United Kingdom needs to follow the example of the majority of its European partners and extend to the women of Britain and Northern Ireland similar rights to those enjoyed by millions of women throughout Europe.

Campaign objectives

Voice for Choice is campaigning for five amendments to current abortion law:

- To allow abortion on the request of a woman up to and including 14 weeks of pregnancy;
- To make abortion available with only one doctor's approval from 15 to 24 weeks under the current criteria;
- To place a duty on doctors to declare any conscientious objection to abortion they may have, and to refer women immediately to another doctor who does not share that view;
- To extend this amended act to Northern Ireland; and
- To place a duty on the National Health Service to provide sufficient abortion services to cover local needs.

A call to action

The parliamentarians who enacted the ground-breaking 1967 legislation, together with other major social reforms of that time, showed great courage and are owed a huge debt of gratitude by every woman who has since found herself facing an unplanned pregnancy. By a single legislative act, by recognising the changing mores of society and the new needs of women in the Sixties, the reformers consigned the harrowing spectre of backstreet butchery into the dim recesses of memory.

However much the Abortion Act improved the position for the women of the Sixties, it is undoubtedly time to move on and frame a law which reflects the greatly changed needs of the women of the Nineties. There should be no place in our society today for a law that discriminates against both individual women and entire groups of women; that encourages confusion about their entitlement under the law; that allows certain individuals the right to impose their will and morality over others; and that risks the physical and emotional health of thousands of women.

All those who believe in freedom of choice and personal autonomy will support the call for abortion law reform.

Add your voice for choice in the Great Britain and Northern Ireland of the next millennium:

- Contact the Pro-Choice Alliance today or send an e-mail to: vfc@mailbox.co.uk
- Write to your MP at the House of Commons, London SW1A 0AA, about your support for a woman's right to choose an abortion and the need for a change in the law.

Rape and abortion

The hard case faced

Rape is a terrible crime against women. The victims need support, sympathy and understanding. Many will need skilled help, perhaps for months or even years afterwards, to try to heal their emotional hurt.

Rape is destructive and violent, and often leaves the victim, the woman, severely damaged. Sometimes she is physically damaged. More often, emotionally. Anger, fear, guilt, disgust and loss of self-esteem will afflict her.

This happens even when there is no pregnancy as a result of rape.

Fortunately it is very rare for a woman to be made pregnant by rape.

Why is pregnancy rare after rape?

There are several reasons:

- The woman may be infertile at the time. She may be in the infertile phase of her monthly cycle, too old or young to conceive, using contraception or sterilised.
- Trauma from the rape may bring into play some natural defence mechanisms that reduce the likelihood of pregnancy, such as hormonal change and spasms of the fallopian tubes which inhibit ovulation or fertilisation.
- Rape does not always involve a complete act of sexual intercourse. Ejaculation may not occur or the rapist may be infertile.

But if she's unlucky and gets pregnant surely it makes sense to have an abortion?

Abortion itself causes problems. It can produce the same kind of anger, fear, guilt, self-doubt that follow rape. LIFE is asked for help by hundreds of women every year who have had abortions and cannot live with their feelings afterwards. For many women abortion, like rape, is an experience they will never forget. After abortion, as well as after rape, women need skilled counselling and help.

Abortion can also cause physical damage. It can cause infertility. It increases the chance of miscarriage and makes sexually transmitted disease, like chlamydia, worse. This doesn't happen very often – but it does happen and there's no guarantee that it won't.

If one dreadful and violent experience – rape – is swiftly followed by another – abortion – what's that going to do to her? We all know what abortion does to the baby. The baby is a new human person – it's not his/her fault that conception occurred in this awful way. Why should he or she be victimised by being killed? Why has he or she less right to life than other people?

But there's another victim in abortion – the mother.

Abortion following rape could leave a woman severely psychologically distressed, perhaps with physical after-effects as well. Is this really the best way for her to be helped?

But surely it would be worse for her to continue pregnancy? Won't she hate the child?

LIFE knows from the women made pregnant by rape whom we have helped when they chose to continue pregnancy that hostile and negative feelings towards the baby change during pregnancy. A few women have even abandoned their plans to have the baby adopted and decided to bring up the baby themselves.

Much depends on other people's attitudes. If a woman has the support and admiration of people round her to help her choose to continue pregnancy, her emotional health will be much stronger than if she suffers the double trauma of abortion after rape. It won't be easy, but she will have the strength that comes from being positive and giving life to her child. Despite the horrible injustice of rape she has refused the further damage to her and the injustice to her child of abortion.

Abortion following rape could leave a woman severely psychologically distressed, perhaps with physical after-effects as well

What about the child? Who wants to be known as the child of a rapist?

Many children have parents who are cruel, criminal, violent. Yet we don't say that those children are worthless. We try to make life better for them. Children conceived in rape are as valuable persons as other children. If they are allowed to live, they will know that their mothers are brave and kind.

Aren't you asking too much from the woman pregnant from rape?

We care for women. We know that abortion damages women, sometimes for ever. We know that in a 'no-win' situation like this we should all try for 'damage limitation'. Abortion won't make the rape not to have happened. On the contrary, it could make matters much worse. Difficult though it is to continue a deeply unwanted pregnancy, the choice for childbirth is a choice to bring something good out of what is horrible and evil. It is a choice that won't harm her as much as abortion, and will allow her to remember her generosity, courage and strength rather than the humiliation and violence of rape followed by abortion.

LIFE has helped – LIFE will help

Over more than twenty years of counselling and care for hundreds of thousands of women LIFE has been asked for help by only a few pregnant as a result of rape. LIFE was able to help them with accommodation away from their area or support and counselling. They ranged in age from 13 to the mid-thirties. At least two decided at the end of pregnancy that they wanted to keep their babies – and LIFE was able to help them with subsequent accommodation.

LIFE'S way is the pro-woman as well as pro-life way.

Our other publications

We publish a wide range of booklets and leaflets on pregnancy, the moral issues involved in abortion, methods of abortion, coping with unwanted pregnancy and disability, LIFE's work in Eastern Europe, etc. – as well as leaflets and posters explaining its nationwide care service for pregnant women and unsupported mothers.

We also produce videos, booklets, posters and wall-charts (especially useful in schools) showing how human life develops in the womb, and Briefing Sheets on the physical and mental effects of abortion, the ethics of embryo research, RU486, etc.

• The above information is from LIFE. See page 41 for their address details.

Morning after pill to be free for 85,000 in scheme to cut abortion

By Auslan Cramb, Scotland Correspondent

More than 85,000 women, aged between 16 and 29, are to be offered free supplies of the 'morning after' pill in an attempt to cut the abortion rate.

The contraception will be made available to women attending 100 GP practices and family planning clinics in the Lothian area, in the biggest experiment of its kind in Britain. Dr Anna Glaister said the pill, which can be taken the day after unprotected sex, was under-used in a part of Scotland in which 12,000 pregnancies were terminated each year.

Dr Glaister, the director of Lothian's family planning service, said: 'Sex often occurs at weekends, and there can often be no time on Mondays to see a doctor.' The move was welcomed by the Royal College of Nursing as a way of tackling unwanted teenage pregnancies but the Catholic Church said it opposed the pill as much as abortion.

A similar scheme announced this summer by the British Pregnancy Advisory Service provoked an outcry amid claims that it would encourage promiscuity. The service's centres offer women emergency supplies of the pill for a £10 charge, following a consultation with a doctor.

But in the trial launched in Edinburgh yesterday, women can ask for up to 20 pills, for use over the next two years. Dr Glaister said the study could prevent 300 abortions.

The scheme has been introduced a year after research suggested that unwanted pregnancies among young women might drop dramatically if they were able to buy the morning after pill across the counter. Dr Glaister previously conducted a study with Prof David Baird, of Edinburgh University, of more than 100 women who had asked for the pill, or had an abortion.

Half were given supplies of the pill to keep in their bathroom cabinets, and half were told to consult their GP. A year later, one-third of the women who had pills at home reported that they had used them in an emergency, while only one in seven from the second group asked a doctor to prescribe the pill.

There were 50 per cent more unwanted pregnancies among the women who had to visit their doctors. Dr Glaister said: 'Women who kept it at home were not more likely to use it repeatedly. They did not abandon more reliable methods of contraception, and the incidence of unwanted pregnancy was reduced.'

'I think we have to be prepared to look at this and discuss openly if it should be changed'

The British Medical Association and the Royal College of Obstetricians and Gynaecologists have supported the idea of emergency contraception being made available over the counter. However, drug companies have been put off applying for such a licence because of opposition from pro-life groups.

Susan Deacon, the Scottish health minister, said a doctor's prescription should be required for emergency contraception, but added: 'I think we have to be prepared to look at this and discuss openly if it should be changed.'

However, Fr Tom Connelly, a spokesman for the Catholic Church, said the morning after pill caused abortion. He said: 'It is murdering somebody, so it is by no means the better of the two evils. The only safe sex is no sex, and sex outside marriage is wrong.

'I challenge young people to be self-disciplined and young men to treat women with respect, and not as objects for personal pleasure. It is outrageous that money can be found to throw around contraceptive pills like this when the NHS cannot find it for people who have actual illnesses.'

Alternatives to abortion

Women who find themselves facing an unwanted pregnancy have two main alternatives to abortion: looking after the baby themselves or allowing it to be adopted

Motherhood – keeping the baby

Some women decide that even though they didn't plan or want this baby, motherhood is the option they would choose.

If a woman is thinking of keeping the baby she needs to ask herself lots of questions. Some of them are:

- Do I feel ready to be a parent?
- What will I do for money?
- Where will I live?
- Will I work? Will I still be able to go to school/college?
- Will the baby's father help?
- What will life be like in one/two/five years' time?
- Will it be very different to how it would have been?
- Will I mind?
- Who will help me towards the end of my pregnancy with practical arrangements?
- How much support will I have from my family and friends?
- How will the baby affect my future relationships?
- What will I have to give up?

If the woman has a partner, talking things over together can help. However, if she feels she cannot rely on the support of the father during the pregnancy and once the baby is born, she needs not only to ask herself all the questions above, but also whether she feels physically and emotionally strong enough to take the place of both parents.

For some women carrying on the pregnancy and keeping the baby is the right choice, especially if they have support from their family and friends. But bringing up a child alone can be very hard:

"Just staying in the house is boring, you don't see anyone or talk to anyone. You get depressed and slouch around. To look after him for three hours is enough for anyone.'

Being married to, or living with, the father just because of the baby does not necessarily make things easier:

'He's realising slowly that there's responsibility and it's not just a case of "I've got a kid" – it's not for show. At first he didn't realise that along with it there comes clothes, buggies, food bills, extras for everything. He's frightened.'

Even some young mothers who are coping well with their new baby have words of caution for other young people:

'Take care not to get yourself in the situation in the first place. I always said that it wouldn't happen to me.'

Adoption

Women who decide they want to give their baby up for adoption need to ask themselves some questions first. They include:

- Can I face going through pregnancy and birth only to give my baby away?
- Will I want to see the baby after the birth?
- Could I cope with knowing I have a child somewhere?
- How will I deal with people who know I've been pregnant and wonder why I haven't got a baby?
- How will I cope at school/work before and after the birth?
- How might my child feel about the fact that they are adopted when they are older?

Adoptions are arranged through the Social Services or Social Work department of the local authority. If a woman decides to have her baby adopted a social worker will discuss with her the kind of people who are going to adopt her baby and make all the necessary arrangements. At some point after the baby is at least six weeks old, the woman will be asked to sign a document giving her agreement that the child can be adopted. The final adoption order only goes ahead once the social worker is satisfied that all is well for the baby in its new home. The woman can change her mind about having her baby adopted at any time before the final adoption order, although if the baby's new family has already applied for adoption an independent assessor from the court will have to be appointed to decide where the baby should stay.

In the past, more babies were adopted because of the shame attached to being an unmarried mother, but now attitudes have changed fewer unmarried mothers feel obliged to give up their baby for adoption. In 1975 4500 babies were put up for adoption, but this figure had fallen to 322 in 1995.

Giving away a child can be a heartbreaking decision and for some women the maternal instinct proves too strong:

'I went to the Adoption Centre twice and then two or three weeks before I was going to have the baby I decided I wanted to keep it . . . I'm glad.'

Abortion worldwide and the population control movement

The United Kingdom

In thirty years after the passing of the 1967 Abortion Act, which applies to England, Wales and Scotland, over 4.5 million abortions were performed in Britain; in the last fifteen years of that period the annual total of abortions exceeded 170,000 – some 500 a day. This is over ten times the number of illegal abortions prior to 1967 according to the most objective estimate (in 1966 the Council of the Royal College of Obstetricians and Gynaecologists offered evidence to indicate that there were some 15,000 illegal abortions a year in England and Wales, whereas the pro-abortion lobby repeatedly claimed that there were 100,000). The Abortion Act does not apply to Northern Ireland.

Although more than 90% of abortions are certified as being done to safeguard the mother's physical or mental health, it is widely recognised that the majority of these abortions are done in response to social rather than medical problems, and that abortion is practised virtually on demand.

Worldwide

It is evident that abortion was practised – by some – from ancient times, from the fact that abortion is prohibited by the Hippocratic Oath, the foundation of medical ethics in the Western world, which was drawn up around 450 BC. However, it is only in recent decades, under pro-abortion laws, that abortion has reached wholesale proportions. There is no reliable, authoritative estimate of the annual number of abortions worldwide: widely quoted estimates of between 40 and 70 million are not, for the most part, based on reliable data.

Abortion and the promotion of contraception

Contraception is an intervention to prevent sexual intercourse from resulting in the union of sperm and ovum (the conception of a child).

SOCIETY FOR THE PROTECTION OF UNBORN CHILDREN

A contraceptive action is thus distinct both from natural methods of family planning which involve no such intervention, and from abortion, which involves an attack on the life of the child after conception (fertilisation) has taken place. (It should be noted, however, that while some methods of birth control, e.g. sterilisation, are solely contraceptive, others, e.g. the mini-pill, also act to cause early abortion and thus attack the right to life of the human embryo.)

The principle of contraception is a question of sexual ethics and, like sexual morality in general, outside SPUC's remit. However, it is within our remit to comment on the promotion of contraception in so far as this affects attitudes to unborn children. Contrary to claims that contraception reduces the demand for abortion, the incidence of abortion is typically high in Western countries where contraception is promoted and widely considered acceptable.

Promoters of birth control for the young have on occasion admitted that such policies facilitate sexual intercourse, with the possibility of pregnancy in circumstances which are not ideal: 'It's partly because of a greater availability of contraception that there are more pregnancies. I suppose it's almost inevitable.' (Jean Malcolm, Brook Advisory Centre Director, *Edinburgh and Lothian Post*, 11.1.92)

The associated high incidence of abortion may in part be attributed to the anti-child mentality which has developed. This often results in a greater keenness to eliminate unplanned babies (regarded as the 'mistakes' of contraceptive failure) than to help expectant mothers avoid abortion.

The population control movement

The largest single vehicle for the promotion of abortion worldwide is the population control movement. The legalisation of abortion has, in many countries, been promoted in the context of alarm about 'overpopulation'. The belief that population growth is the cause of poverty, famine and environmental degradation has been used to justify the exercising of state control over family size. Population control is in itself an infringement of human rights, and also facilitates attacks on the right to life of unborn children.

Population control versus family planning

By referring to population control measures as 'family planning', population control advocates have confused the issue. Family planning, in its true sense, is a fundamentally different concept to population control. Population control involves decisions taken by governments or other agencies regarding the number of children couples ought to have, followed by measures to bring this about. Family planning, by contrast, involves decisions made by couples themselves regarding the number and spacing of their children. It is the right and responsibility of couples, and of no one else, to make these decisions. SPUC opposes population control programmes as an attack on the freedom of couples which is fundamentally anti-child.

Those promoting population control often claim that they seek only to satisfy the 'unmet need for family planning' of women in developing countries. In reality, measures to reduce population always involve pressure or coercion, whether through media propaganda, financial incentives, peer group pressure, intimidation or force. Furthermore, some commentators have identified abortion as a critical factor in population growth control.

Forced abortion in China

The Chinese population control programme is the most notorious in the world. Chinese government economic policy has had disastrous effects on the country's agricultural system, particularly the major famines of the late 1950s, which have been falsely attributed to population growth. Since 1979-1980, shortly after the policy of one child per family was introduced, the Chinese government's population control programme has been supported by the assistance of the United Nations Population Fund (UNFPA) and the International Planned Parenthood Federation (IPPF), despite abundant evidence of forced abortion and sterilisation. Chinese law refers to abortion 'as required by the family planning programme'. The programme has resulted in the resurgence of female infanticide in China (causing an imbalance in the male/female ratio and thus seriously affecting fertility rates), a situation compounded by the 'dying rooms' of state-run orphanages where female and disabled infants are left to die of neglect.

In spite of the fact that the UNFPA and IPPF give assistance to the Chinese population programme, and are leading advocates for the programme internationally, Western governments (notably Britain) continue to give substantial grants of taxpayers' money to both of these organisations.

The United Nations

Recent United Nations Conferences – on population, social development, the status of women, urban settlements, food and the environment – have been platforms for attempts by wealthy nations to impose abortion and population control on developing countries. The rationale for this appears to be, in part, the ideological commitment of the population control lobby, and economic self-interest on the part of Western governments. National delegates opposed to abortion on demand and to population control have had some success in amending pro-abortion language in conference documents, which do not have force of law but are used to exert pressure on developing countries which have signed them.

The attack on the young

The population control lobby is also promoting, through the United Nations and through organisations at national level, the provision of abortion and birth control to adolescents (including those under the age of consent to sexual intercourse) without parental knowledge or consent. For example, the Brook Advisory Centres, which pioneered abortion referrals and contraceptive provision to adolescents in Britain, began as an offshoot of the Family Planning Association, one of the founding member organisations of the International Planned Parenthood Federation.

Young girls are particularly vulnerable to pressure to undergo abortion. This is a danger inherent in underage sexual intercourse, which is facilitated and made to appear 'safe' by the provision of contraception. There is evidence – which officers of the Brook Advisory Centres have on occasion acknowledged – that the provision of birth control to the young has aggravated the rise in underage conceptions and abortions. The practice of bypassing parental consent is opposed by SPUC as an anti-family policy which is demonstrably against the interests of unborn children.

Certain forms of sex education which promote such practices also contribute greatly to the problem. They should be replaced by approaches which respect the dignity of young people, the rights and responsibilities of parents and the inalienable right to life of the unborn baby.

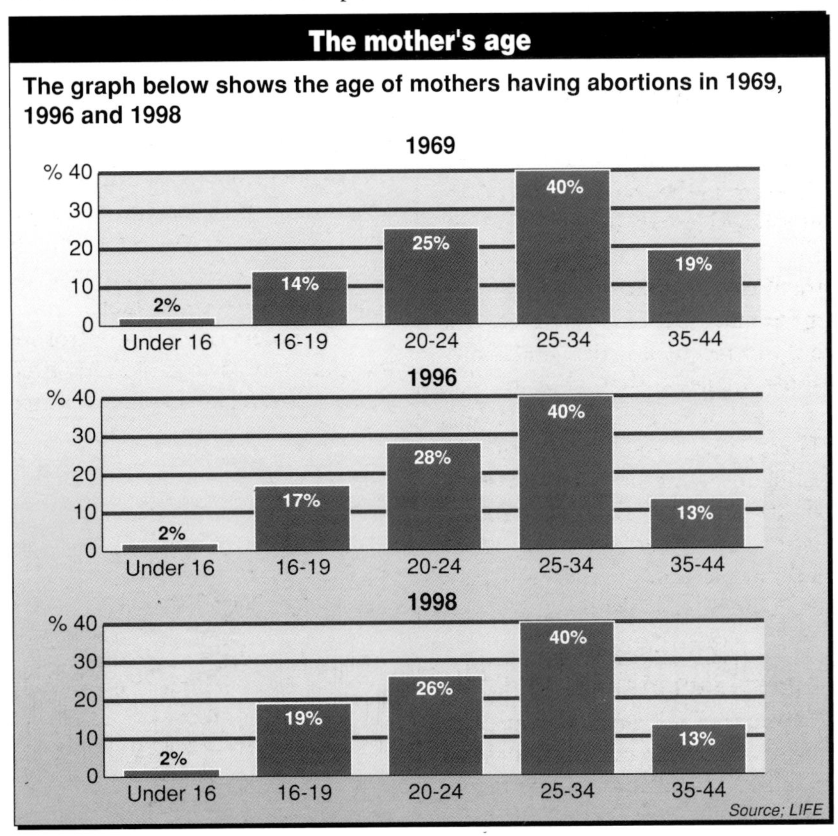

Abortion in the developing world

Information from the World Health Organisation (WHO)

Out of nearly 50 million abortions performed in the world each year (30 million of them in developing countries), 20 million are unsafe, according to a World Health Organisation (WHO) publication *Abortion in the Developing World*.

Close to 90%of all unsafe abortions take place in developing countries. In 94% of these countries, induced abortion is restricted by law. The risk of dying from an unsafe abortion in a developing country is 1 in 250 procedures, while in developed countries it is 1 in 3,700 procedures.

Induced abortions, especially in countries where the practice is restricted by law, continue to be a major reproductive health problem. Some 70,000 women die each year as a result of unsafe abortion. Many more women survive the experience only to suffer throughout the rest of their lives from infertility, chronic morbidity and permanent physical impairment.

A strong motivation to seek an abortion rests on the widespread desire for smaller families, the need to control the timing of births and the failure or inconsistent use of contraception. Poor access to family planning services, shifts from rural to urban settings, poverty and hardship, increase in non-marital sexual activity, adolescent sexuality coupled with unprotected sex, all contribute to the continuing practice of abortion in the developing world.

The case studies included in the book and conducted in countries as far apart as Mexico and Mauritius, China and Cuba, suggest that the relationship between contraceptive needs and induced abortion remains, for the most part, unexplored territory in reproductive health research. For most women in the developing world, where abortion is usually restricted and unsafe, contraception would seem to offer a better fertility regulation option. Yet the research findings indicate the extensive use of induced abortion even in countries with good family planning services.

Induced abortion exists everywhere, both in countries where family planning programmes are strong as well as where they are weak or non-existent. Often enough, it occurs within marriage to limit family size. Thus, in the Nepal study, unplanned pregnancy accounted for 95% of induced abortion but the majority of women were not using contraception.

In the Dominican Republic scarcely 25% of women were using a contraceptive method when they became pregnant unintentionally. Even in China, where contraception is easily and widely available, non-use of contraception is a primary reported reason for unwanted pregnancy and abortion. However, contraceptive failure can go as high as 37% (China), as the reported reason for abortion. In the Cuba study, three out of every four women who had had an abortion in the last 12 months reported using a modern method of contraceptive at the time they were surveyed.

Based on several studies, researchers concluded that non-use and low continuation of use of modern contraceptive methods among the women who had an abortion in developing countries resulted from the women's negative perception of contraceptives, especially hormonal ones, which they felt had side effects and lacked in safety.

Whatever the complexities of the relationship between contraception and abortion, all the studies call for general improvement in the quality of reproductive health services as a way to reduce the recourse to abortion. There is an urgent need to make available a wider range of contraceptive methods to allow users greater freedom to choose what suits their needs best. Ensuring longer continuation of use is one way of lowering abortion risks among women who do not want to become pregnant.

Abortion continues to be a very controversial and complex issue given its political, religious, ethical and health dimensions which often lead to heated debates in public forums. The book sheds new light on the reality of abortion which varies dramatically in different social, legal and political contexts.

ADDITIONAL RESOURCES

You might like to contact the following organisations for further information. Due to the increasing cost of postage, many organisations cannot respond to enquiries unless they receive a stamped, addressed envelope.

The Abortion Law Reform Association (ALRA)
2-12 Pentonville Road
London, N1 9FP
Tel: 020 7278 5539
Fax: 020 7278 5236
E-mail: alra@mailbox.co.uk
Web site: www.alra.mailbox.co.uk
The Abortion Law Reform Association believes women should be allowed to make up their own minds on abortion, regardless of their circumstances.

British Humanist Association
47 Theobald's Road
London, WC1X 8SP
Tel: 020 7430 0908
Fax: 020 7430 1271
E-mail: info@humanism.org.uk
Web site: www.humanism.org.uk
The British Humanist Association is the UK's leading organisation for people concerned with ethics and society, free from religious and supernatural dogma. Publishes a wide range of free briefings.

British Pregnancy Advisory Service (BPAS)
Austy Manor, Wootton Wawen
Solihull
West Midlands, B95 6BX
Tel: 01564 793225
Fax: 01564 794935
E-mail: comm.@bpas.org
Web site: www.bpas.org
BPAS supports reproductive choice by advocating and providing high-quality, affordable services to prevent or end unwanted pregnancy with contraception or by abortion. Runs the BPAS Abortion Actionline. To make an appointment phone 08457 304030.

Brook Advisory Centres
Studio 421, Highgate Studios
51-79 Highgate Road
London, NW5 1TL
Tel: 020 7284 6040
Fax: 020 7284 6050
Web site: www.brook.org.uk
Brook is a professional non-profit making organisation for young people up to the age of 25. It exists to enable all young people to make informed choices about their personal and sexual relationships so that they can enjoy their sexuality without harm. Runs a helpline on 0800 0185 023.

CARE (Christian Action Research and Education)
53 Romney Street
London, SW1P 3RF
Tel: 020 7233 0455
Fax: 020 7233 0983
E-mail: info@care.org.uk
Web site: www.care.org.uk
A Christian charity which produces a wide range of publications presenting a Christian perspective on moral issues. Ask for their Resources Catalogue.

Christian Medical Fellowship (CMF)
157 Waterloo Road
London, SE1 8XN
Tel: 020 7928 4694
Fax: 020 7620 2453
E-mail: admin@cmf.org.uk
Web site: www.cmf.org.uk
A network of approximately 4,500 doctors and 600 medical students throughout the UK and Republic of Ireland. They produce a range of booklets and leaflets.

Education for Choice (EFC)
2-12 Pentonville Road
London, N1 9FP
Tel: 020 7837 7221
Fax: 020 7254 7838
E-mail: efc@efc.org.uk
Web site: www.efc.org.uk
Education for Choice believes that abortion is morally and medically acceptable. Produces a factsheet and education pack.

LIFE
LIFE House, Newbold Terrace
Leamington Spa
Warwickshire, CV32 4EA
Tel: 01926 421587
Fax: 01926 336497
E-mail: info@lifeuk.org
Web site: www.lifeuk.org
LIFE provides a nationwide care service for pregnant girls and women – as well as for unsupported mothers, women with problems relating to pregnancy, fertility or infertility, or suffering from the effects of abortion. Produces publications.

Marie Stopes International
153-157 Cleveland Street
London, WIP 5PG
Tel: 020 7574 7400
E-mail: service@stopes.org.uk
Web site: www.mariestopes.org.uk
Provides reproductive healthcare, family planning services and information, to enable individuals all over the world to have children by choice, not by chance. Produces publications.

National Abortion Campaign (NAC)
The Print House
18 Ashwin Street
London, E8 3DL
Tel: 020 7923 4976
E-mail: nac@gn.apc.org
Web site: www.gn.apc.org/nac
NAC is a member organisation which campaigns for safe, free abortion on request for all women who want one. Produces publications.

ProLife Alliance
PO Box 13395
London, SW3 6XE
Tel: 020 7351 9955
E-mail: info@prolifealliance.org.uk
Web site: www.prolifealliance.org.uk
Seeks to ensure the right to life of all, the most basic and fundamental human right.

Society for the Protection of Unborn Children (SPUC)
Phyllis Bowman House
5-6 St Matthew Street
Westminster, London, SW1P 2 JT
Tel: 020 7222 5845
E-mail: enquiry@spuc.org.uk
Web site: www.spuc.org.uk
SPUC defends the human rights of the child in the womb. They also campaign against other threats to the right to live.

INDEX

Independence Web News

Back | Forward | Home | Reload | Images | Open | Print | Find | Stop

Live Home Page | Search | Computer | Support | System

*****

The Internet has been likened to shopping in a supermarket without aisles. The press of a button on a Web browser can bring up thousands of sites but working your way through them to find what you want can involve long and frustrating on-line searches. And unfortunately many sites contain inaccurate, misleading or heavily biased information. Our researchers have therefore undertaken an extensive analysis to bring you a selection of quality Web site addresses.

The Abortion Law Reform Association (ALRA)
www.alra.org.uk
The Abortion Law Reform Association believes women should be allowed to make up their own minds on abortion, regardless of their circumstances. This web site contains information on abortion including: Effects of Abortion, Abortion Law in the UK, NHS Abortion Provision and Further Information.

British Pregnancy Advisory Service (BPAS)
www.bpas.org
Click on Facts And Stats for a range of informative articles.

Education for Choice
www.efc.org.uk
Education For Choice is a charity that provides education and training resources on abortion from a pro-choice perspective. Useful information.

Alliance for Choice
members.aol.com/~choiceni/
Alliance for Choice is an organisation of Catholics and Protestants, women and men, campaigning for the extension of the 1967 Abortion Act to Northern Ireland. Although they differ in their approach to the constitutional question, they all agree that as long as NI remains part of the United Kingdom, women there should have the same rights as women in the rest of the UK. This web site covers the situation in Ireland and offers information on obtaining an abortion.

Society for the Protection of Unborn Children (SPUC)
www.spuc.org.uk
SPUC was launched in 1967 to campaign against the Abortion Act. As the first 'right to life' lobbying and educational organisation established anywhere in the world, the Society defends the human rights of the child in the womb. This web site covers The Unborn Child, Topical Issues, News, SPUC's Work, Help and Advice and Links.

LIFE
www.lifeuk.org
Provides a nationwide care service for pregnant women, unsupported mothers, women with problems relating to pregnancy, fertility or infertility, or suffering from the effects of abortion. Clicking on Information for Students there is a choice of GCSE, In-Depth and Educational Services. The GCSE link is information intended for students just beginning to investigate abortion and other 'life' issues. It is appropriate for GCSE (or Scottish SCE) R.S. and P.S.E./P.S.H.E coursework.

Christian Medical Fellowship (CMF)
www.cmf.org.uk
CMF produces literature addressing a wide range of ethical issues from a Christian perspective. The Site Index provides links to articles on numerous ethical topics including abortion.

ACKNOWLEDGEMENTS

The publisher is grateful for permission to reproduce the following material.

While every care has been taken to trace and acknowledge copyright, the publisher tenders its apology for any accidental infringement or where copyright has proved untraceable. The publisher would be pleased to come to a suitable arrangement in any such case with the rightful owner.

Chapter One: An Overview

Abortion facts, © Marie Stopes International, *Answering young people's questions on abortion*, © Brook Advisory Centres, *Religion and abortion*, © Education for Choice, *Abortion and the Catholic Church*, © Catholic Media Office, *Unwanted pregnancy and abortion*, © Abortion Law Reform Association (ALRA), *Abortion law*, © British Pregnancy Advisory Service (BPAS), *Women in 30s 'still failing on contraception'*, © Telegraph Group Limited, London 2000, *Abortion methods*, © British Pregnancy Advisory Service (BPAS), *Men and abortion*, © Christian Action Research and Education (CARE).

Chapter Two: The Right to Choose?

Abortion: an introduction, © Education for Choice, *Opinions on abortion*, © British Pregnancy Advisory Service (BPAS), *Opinions on abortion*, © British Pregnancy Advisory Service (BPAS), *Ethical consideration of abortion*, © British Medical Association (BMA), *Matters of life and death*, © The ProLife Alliance, *Abortion*, © Education for Choice, *Grounds for abortion*, © Office for National Statistics (ONS), *A non-religious perspective on abortion*, © British Humanist Association (BHA), *A woman's right to choose?*, © LIFE, *8 myths about abortion*, © National Abortion Campaign (NAC), *Key issue – abortion*, © Society for the Protection of Unborn Children (SPUC), *Questions you ask about abortion*, © National Abortion Campaign (NAC), *Deadly questions*, © Christian Medical Fellowship (CMF), *Anti-choice questions: Pro-choice answers*, © National Abortion Campaign (NAC), *Young girls need facts*, © Guardian Newspapers Limited, 2000, *At what gestation do most abortions occur?*, © British Pregnancy Advisory Service (BPAS), *Most GPs 'now back abortion on demand'*, © Telegraph Group Limited, London 2000, *Abortion guidelines hailed by campaigners*, © Guardian Newspapers Limited, 2000, *Family planning group shatters 'A' word taboo*, © Telegraph Group Limited, London 2000, *Women versus babies*, © Guardian Newspapers Limited, 2000, *Voice for choice*, © Voice for Choice, *Rape and abortion*, © LIFE, *Morning after pill to be free for 85,000 in scheme to cut abortion*, © Telegraph Group Limited, London 2000, *Alternatives to abortion*, © Education for Choice, *Abortion worldwide and the population control movement*, © Society for the Protection of Unborn Children (SPUC), *The mother's age*, © LIFE, *Abortion in the developing world*, © WHO/OMS.

Photographs and illustrations:

Pages 1, 6, 11, 14, 19, 30, 37: Pumpkin House, pages 23, 26, 34, 40: Simon Kneebone.

Craig Donnellan
Cambridge
September, 2000